Philosopher
at the
Keyboard:

GLENN GOULD

by
ELIZABETH ANGILETTE

The Scarecrow Press, Inc.
Metuchen, N.J., & London
1992

This book is based on the author's doctoral dissertation, "Glenn Gould (1932–1982): A Study of His Contribution to a Philosophy of Music and Music Education," New York University, 1988.

British Library Cataloguing-in-Publication data available

Library of Congress Cataloging-in-Publication Data

Angilette, Elizabeth, 1945–
    Philosopher at the keyboard, Glenn Gould / by Elizabeth Angilette.
        p.   cm.
    Includes bibliographical references and indexes.
    ISBN 0-8108-2467-1 (acid-free paper)
    1. Gould, Glenn—Philosophy.   2. Music—Philosophy and aesthetics. I. Title.
ML417.G68A8   1992
786.2'092—dc20   91-42986

*For all musicians
who use their art
to ennoble the human spirit*

CONTENTS

FOREWORD

Elizabeth Angilette has studied systematically Glenn Gould's available books, articles, media narratives, lectures, program notes, and even marginalia. Her book's historical importance is due largely to the rigorous review of Gould's richly divergent written works. Such an overview and presentation is not an easy accomplishment because of Gould's highly idiosyncratic discursive style. However, the assimilation and presentation of Gould's huge and thematically kaleidoscopic corpus was only a starting point for Dr. Angilette. In this book she has uncovered philosophical, educational, and sociological themes and has brought them together in an original account of the overall intellectual and musical thrust of Gould's thoughts.

Angilette clearly sides with those Gould scholars and critics who have concluded that there is coherence, rationality, and substance in his output. This position is not held universally. Many detractors of Gould's written works have judged them to be, at best, insightful but highly subjective. That is to say, while his work makes for interesting reading, they would say it lacks the rigor that is required of scholarship. Other detractors have argued further that much of Gould's written work can be regarded as mere gibberish. Angilette's study gives cause to reconsider these negative interpretations.

The present book might have dealt exclusively with uncovering the underlying logic and themes in Gould's works; such a project—discovering and establishing that his works are systematic, coherent, clear, and insightful—would have, in itself, made Angilette's work worthwhile. However, she goes beyond such a review and clarification. She has operationalized her analyses of Gould's works by bridging them with existing philosophies of music and music education as well as the sociological aspects of these disciplines. In order to construct such a bridge, Angilette reviewed the extant literature that presents philosophical and sociological accounts of music and music education. While an exhaustive review of that related literature is beyond the scope of any single volume, Angilette's selection of sources is representative of the literature as it bears upon her study. Thus, many interesting and cogent discussions are presented concerning the status of Gould's work and its usefulness in the ongoing development of philosophies and sociologies of music and music education.

Angilette's book is also important because of its utilization of an eclectic methodology. She has juxtaposed historical and philosophical methods. Most historical accounts tend to bypass philosophical issues. At the same time, philosophical studies of music and music education rarely engage strict historical explanation. The eclectic methodological approach conceived and implemented in this study contributes an important model for subsequent historical studies, particularly in music education. Moreover and more specific to this study, this eclecticism provides a necessary methodological responsiveness to the multiplicity of ideas and issues articulated in Gould's thematically kaleidoscopic works. It is only through such an approach that the variety and scope of his writings can be sufficiently and successfully studied.

Historical accounts strive for factual rigor. In this way, they present a commensurate degree of verifiable or corroborable evidence. One might term the aggregate of these historical facts in a study its "inevitable" dimension. "Inevitability" refers to what is readily corroborable through historical method. But Angilette has also injected philosophical inquiry into her largely historical study. The data that has been extrapolated from her philosophical exegeses and comparatives are not readily afforded the status of "inevitable" facts. Unlike more traditional formal and historical methods used in research in music and music education, philosophical inquiry does not rely so much on factual, corroborable, or "inevitable" data but provides insights that result from interpretation. One can call this second type of database "inventive." This philosophical dimension of the database cannot achieve the corroborability or "inevitability" that marks historical facts. Nevertheless, Angilette's philosophical or "inventive" database grounds, clarifies, and enriches many of the historical facts presented throughout the study.

In a study such as this, the "inevitable" and "inventive" dimensions of data collection and synthesis must be balanced. A strict historical account of Gould's works would not uncover his many metaphorical presentations of ideas and positions. But in any scholarly study, one must not allow poetic license to obscure factual content. Thus, an underlying dialectic must occur that regulates the contrapuntal force of the historically and philosophically based data. In this respect, Angilette's study is successful. Her juxtaposition of these two methodologies is executed carefully. This requires an understanding of both methods that is marked by appreciation. Appreciation does not connote liking or disliking, approving or disapproving. Rather, it is a mode of orientation that seeks to understand the underlying logic and structures, the implicit and explicit guidelines and protocols, and the overall thrust of one's method or subject.

Angilette's appreciative understanding and utilization of historical and philosophical methods have allowed her to be more responsive to the content in Gould's writings. His corpus is constituted of a rich mixture of fact and comment, "inevitability" and "inventiveness." While some of his writings can be evaluated and rated as being more or less historically factual, much of it must be interpreted and clarified through philosophical analysis. Indeed, consideration of the fecundity of many of Gould's positions most often requires movement to their underlying philosophical grounds. For example, Gould concluded that technology should be used overtly to improve recorded performances. Specifically, he contended that performers should work with recording engineers closely in order to dub, splice, and insert sections from several recorded performances into a final recorded performance for the public. While his position can be reported factually as it appears in his published works, there is a philosophical issue at work as well. Musical performance is marked not only by technical control and stylistic rigor. In addition, it must present those "inevitable" notes in the musical score and learned stylistic norms in a spontaneous, free, or in a word, "inventive" fashion. When engineering is as intrusive as the kind recommended by Gould, the Gould scholar must consider the philosophical impact that such a position might have on the commonly held principle that in order to be successful, a performance must demonstrate a balance and harmony between technical control and freedom. Furthermore, one must ask how this position (and other such positions) held and articulated by Gould fits within, embellishes, and develops current philosophies and sociological accounts of music and music education. This study goes very far in answering these philosophical questions while providing an historically factualist basis for understanding Gould's positions.

Lawrence Ferrara
New York University

ACKNOWLEDGMENTS

I extend my sincere thanks to the following people whose support helped to make this book possible: Dr. Lawrence Ferrara of New York University for his encouragement and advice; Dr. Gabriel Moran of the Religion Studies Program at New York University for his cogent criticism; Dr. Stephen Willis and the entire staff of the Music Division at the National Library of Canada for their ready help; the Canadian Embassy in Washington, D.C., for a fellowship to research Glenn Gould in Canada; the Estate of Glenn Gould for permission to use the Glenn Gould Collection; Ms. Karen Kirshner for her encouragement and help; and finally, my parents, Pauline and Salvatore Angilette, who never failed to enthusiastically support the early expressions of my musical curiosity.

ELIZABETH ANGILETTE
Freeport, New York

1. INTRODUCTION

Since the time of his death in 1982, Glenn Gould has been the subject of a plethora of articles, books, festivals, and special media productions. These projects, no doubt, endeavor to promote a better understanding of Gould and his contributions to music and culture.

However, it appears that Glenn Gould continues to be perceived as an enigma. The genius apparent in his performances is not easily reconciled with the seemingly disparate, at times nonsensical, utterances he made in his writings. These works, the product of much time and toil, are scattered in articles, liner notes, media scripts, lectures, books, and program notes. Most pieces are published in popular publications where Gould shaped his writing style in order to reach the general reader. His style was at times dramatic, polemic, outrageous, and even shocking.

On the surface, Gould appears to be a flamboyant entertainer voicing highly personal, and perhaps inconsequential, opinions on an assortment of subjects. One is forced to wonder, Was he really serious about his work outside of piano performance? Was he actually a troubled mind who squandered his pianistic genius on trivial pursuits? Or did he have something of consequence and value to communicate to the world?

Throughout this book, it is illustrated that, although Gould's thought is marked by a kaleidoscopic range of ideas, closer examination reveals persistent philosophical themes that emerge into a unity of expression. Here, Gould is regarded as more than a great pianist. He is recognized for his serious devotion to creativity, thought, and education. Like Koscis (1983) and Payzant (1978) this author sympathetically recognizes Glenn Gould as a philos-

1

opher of music who used the piano and other media to
convey his thought.

Gould's writings, with their extended paragraphs, frequent asides, and long phrases, work towards a grand line
of expression in form and content. He attempted to
restructure and reorder the musician's creative experience. He showed how the musician can be transformed
and spiritually fulfilled. He redefined the significance of
the artistic experience, unmasked blocks to creativity and
spiritual growth, and ultimately spoke to what he interpreted as the emerging spirit of our times.

Ironically, there appear to be more nonmusicians drawn
to Gould's thought than professional artists. Musicians,
particularly pianists, caught up in a specialist's narrow way
of life and vision might miss the import of Gould's meaning
(Wait, 1986). They might dismiss Gould's thought as trivial
because of the commonly accepted portrait of Gould as an
eccentric.

GOULD AS EDUCATOR

Gould was an example of a musical artist turned educator,
in that he communicated or taught his ideas via writings
and several media. A constant personal need to examine
music in many different contexts was at the root of these
ideas. Music was not to be taken at face value but
investigated, searched for greater meaning and understanding.

In order to achieve his personal and professional goals
more effectively, Gould retreated from the life of a
performing concert pianist to a unique isolation that he felt
was necessary for him to control his creative life (Littler,
1983). Away from the ordinary demands of people, he
channeled his energy into media and writing projects.
These projects resulted in finding and utilizing new ideas
for an arts-media-technology dialogue (Roberts, 1983).

There are over two hundred recordings in Gould's
discography, three published compositions, nine radio
documentaries, and eighteen films in which Gould either

produced, composed, or performed the music (McGreevy, 1983), and well over two hundred citations in the *Music Index* by or about Gould.

Gould's activity with the media linked philosophical speculation, which is grounded in facets of contemporary music, to a musical and educational future in technology. In the words of Denis Dutton, ". . . he [Gould] cannot be ignored by anyone interested in the future of music" (Dutton, 1979).

Gould was a remarkable man of the future in that he was one of the greatest practitioner-catalysts of a philosophy of music that uses radical, iconoclastic notions. These aesthetic thoughts question, even shake, every traditional musical and social footing. The artistic product of such thought serves greater social, political, spiritual, and psychological ends.

Although Gould never thought of himself as an educator, Tim Page (1984), editor of *The Glenn Gould Reader*, asserted that Gould was a born teacher who used the media as his classroom. Gould stimulated the minds of his vast student audience by questioning and probing for greater understanding of musical phenomena. He was a catalyst for the student to learn to think of music in broad, all-encompassing ways. He philosophically stimulated one to question all in the name of truth, wisdom, and goodness.

Indeed, Gould's class, composed of an international audience, presented far greater creative teaching possibilities than any conventional learning institution could offer. Gould believed that the world was the real educator of music. This learning scenario poses a striking resemblance to Marshall McLuhan's vision of learning in the global village (McLuhan, 1969). It is there that traditional education yields to learning obtained in the greater world. It is a learning in a deschooled milieu where the role of the teacher is greatly enriched and expanded (Illich, 1971).

Formal institutions like schools, colleges, and universities were too limiting in their day-to-day operations for Gould's creative mind. And he would most likely agree with Murphy (1980) that music education occurs most from informal institutions, like the media, rather than formal training centers. It is interesting to note that, in spite of his criticism of formal institutions, Gould occasionally lectured in academic and nonacademic settings throughout the world, which included the Moscow Conservatory, several Canadian and American colleges, conservatories, museums, and schools. There he communicated his artistic and intellectual insights that included an exploration of an inner life and mind (McGreevy, 1983).

In Canada, Gould was well known as a media personality who was as magnetic an educator as the American composer-conductor Leonard Bernstein (Gould, 1966d). Gould explained, clarified, and taught through the use of fused musical and media techniques. His strategy of patterning intellectual prose after musical structures was similar to the techniques of Claude Lévi-Strauss who modeled his writings after musical forms like theme and variations, sonata, symphony, and fugue.

Gould's projects took form in radio documentaries, the development of fictitious stock characters, videotapes, films, recordings, lectures, and dialogue essays. Every project was dedicated to new possibilities for music. Indeed, Robert Silverman (1983) understood Gould's future significance when he said that aside from Guild's unique musical performances he will be remembered as one of the century's outstanding philosophical minds.

THE MUSICIAN/PHILOSOPHER/EDUCATOR

Music's most ardent expositors are not necessarily professional philosophers well versed in philosophical speculation, but those to whom music means the most, namely its composers and performers. These are individuals who have scaled to the top of the musical profession, oftentimes, overcoming seemingly insurmountable difficulties. They write impassioned narratives about music and its value in the world.

The practitioners, turned educator-communicators, are often inspired to write about music from a personal need to know why and how music claims such power in their lives.

Examples of this kind of writing can be found in the work of Roger Sessions, Igor Stravinsky, and Glenn Gould.

Roger Sessions asked questions like, "Why have serious and gifted men—in imaginative force and intellectual mastery the equals of any that ever lived—why have such men at all periods devoted their lives to music and found in it a supremely satisfying medium of expression?" (Sessions, 1971, p. 3). He further queried, "We regard music as important, as vitally connected with ourselves and our fate as human beings. But what is the nature of our vital connection with it?" (Sessions, 1971, p. 4).

The musician/philosopher/educator typically explores musical meaning in order to gain an understanding of the nature of music and how it relates to the other dimensions of life. In "The Psychology of Improvisation" Glenn Gould questioned the values and premises upon which people make judgments about art. He concluded that, perhaps, music could have no meaning (Gould, 1966d, p. 255).

Igor Stravinsky wrote, "A composer's work *is* the embodiment of his feelings and, of course, it may be considered as expressing or symbolizing them" (Stravinsky and Craft, 1962, p. 101). He further said, ". . . my objection to music criticism is that it usually directs itself to what it supposes to be the nature of the imitation—when it should be teaching us to learn and to love the new reality. A new piece of music *is* a new reality" (Stravinsky and Craft, 1962, p. 102).

Although the works of musician/philosopher/educators are generally serious endeavors, it is apparent that they seldom probe musical/philosophical problems in a complete, systematic way. These writings do not possess the depth and scope of systematic philosophical work that develops comprehensive theory. The question arises, Do these eclectic, underdeveloped expressions about music possess any value for the philosophical process?

Indeed, Schantz (1983) and Epperson (1967) claimed that no such comprehensive philosophy of music exists. Since no complete philosophical theory of music exists, works that contribute toward its development are certainly noteworthy.

Glenn Gould's thought can be viewed as part of a

continuum of musician/philosopher/educators' work that potentially adds to greater musical theory. And specifically, what significance do Gould's writings have for the development of a philosophy of music and music education? It is hoped that, through an examination of the dominant philosophical themes in Gould's written output, one may arrive at a greater understanding of Glenn Gould and his potential contribution to this development.

THE DEVELOPMENT OF A PHILOSOPHY OF MUSIC AND MUSIC EDUCATION

What does the development of a philosophy of music and music education mean, and what significance does it have for this study? In order to answer these questions it is advantageous to consider the definition of the word "develop."

"Develop" implies that one should advance the growth and evolution of something that one wishes to develop. One should enlarge the capabilities or possibilities of the thing being developed. Ideally, this will evolve it to a more advanced or effective state (Urdang & Flexner, 1968).

The development of a philosophy of music and music education refers to the identification of those metatheoretical features about philosophy that could possibly facilitate and help generate the future growth of a viable, comprehensive philosophical theory of music and music education. It will be demonstrated in this book how Glenn Gould's ideas implement the points in focus concerning this development. The points in focus incisively disclose only the considered philosophies' fundamental dimensions, problems, and issues.

2. THE MUSICAL AND EDUCATIONAL LIFE OF GLENN GOULD

A thorough biographical sketch is needed to weave an account of Gould's dominant ideas around an outline of his life's events. Gould's daily routine was inexorably bound to the pursuit of his ideals. He ignored mundane aspirations in order to pursue his interests with a curious mixture of vigor and abandon. Geoffrey Payzant (1978), Gould's seminal biographer, stated that the best route to understand Gould is to study his ideas since Gould's life was essentially a life of the mind.

Gould's life is compared with the cloistered monk who denies life's ordinary ambitions in order to focus his entire energies on a higher calling. For Gould this meant a unique, solitary journey of an inner existence marked by genius that took on metaphysical, moral, and artistic proportions. Yehudi Menuhin wrote in a final tribute, "So great was the compulsion of his creative universe that he himself (the Glenn that one might but did not touch) was a very touching, tender and extremely sensitive, almost heart-rending, offering—a sacrifice on the altar of his own genius . . ." (Menuhin, 1983, p. 304).

EARLY YEARS

Glenn Gould was born in Toronto, Ontario, on September 25, 1932. He was the only child of Bert, a prosperous furrier, and Florence Gould. Both parents were classical music enthusiasts who were serious about music's value and importance. His mother taught voice, piano, and organ. His father was an amateur violinist.

Like many unusually gifted children, Glenn exhibited

7

exceptional musical qualities from an early age. At three he showed that he possessed absolute pitch as well as the ability to read staff notation. At that time he began his piano studies with his mother, who remained his sole music teacher until he was ten years old.

At five years of age Glenn composed and performed his own compositions. Geoffrey Payzant wrote of one such performance,

> A lady of advanced years gives an eyewitness account of an occasion when he [Gould] came with his mother to perform some of these pieces at the meeting of the Women's Missionary Society at Emmanuel Presbyterian Church, a few blocks from the Gould house. The lady remembers that Glenn was attired in a white satin suit with short pants and charmed the ladies. (Payzant, 1978, p. 2)

In spite of Gould's apparent abilities as a child performer, his parents protected him from the life of a child prodigy by keeping his public performances to a minimum. One of the few exceptions was his participation in the Kiwanis Music Festivals held annually in Toronto. His performance regimen was controlled and developed very gradually. His early talent was nurtured in a private, mutually supportive home that afforded him every opportunity to develop his unusual gifts. According to Robert Fulford, a well-known Canadian writer and early childhood friend of Gould, the family spent about $3,000 a year in 1940's currency on Gould's musical education (Gould, 1983a). He was given the freedom to pursue his musical interests in depth without outside pressures. These activities sometimes took the form of experiments in composition, unusually long practice hours at the piano that often extended into the early morning hours, and listening to live or taped radio broadcasts of music. From an early age Gould was totally absorbed by and dedicated to music.

It is written that

> Even as a child Glenn was isolated because he was working like hell to be a great man. He had a tremendous feeling and loving affection for music. . . . It was an utter complete

feeling. He knew who he was and where he was going. (Bester, 1964, p. 150)

Obviously, he carried his productive learning habits of intense involvement and concentration from early childhood into adulthood. In a film about Gould produced by Vincent Tovell, Gould's father comments that as a child Gould would retreat into his bedroom to learn an unfamiliar musical score. Gould would not return out of his room until he committed the entire score for memory. (Tovell, 1985)

Gould's childhood was dominated by music. During his last years at the Williamson Road Public School he was attending class part-time so that he could spend much of his day at the Toronto Conservatory (Gould, 1983a).

By the time he was ten years old, Gould could play the complete Book I of J. S. Bach's *Well-Tempered Clavier*. He also began his musical studies at the Toronto Conservatory of Music, later renamed the Royal Conservatory of Music. There he studied organ with Frederick C. Silvester, piano with Alberto Guerrero, and music theory with Leo Smith. Gould's extraordinary progress in his studies was demonstrated by his quick mastery of the highest levels of achievement.

According to John Beckwith, also a former Guerrero pupil, Gould was greatly influenced by the Chilean-Canadian pianist-teacher; he adopted several aspects of Guerrero's piano style including the low sitting position at the keyboard, the flat-finger articulation, and the fluency and clarity of rapid finger passages.

Gould also acquired Guerrero's "pure finger technique" as opposed to "weight technique." Gould believed that the rebound in piano technique was closer to what actually happens in playing than theories about "free-fall weight" technique (Silverman, correspondence to the author, dated December 2, 1984). This also reflects the theories of Otto Ortmann, on whom Guerrero based much of his teaching.

Besides Gould and Beckwith, Guerrero also taught several other prominent Canadian composers, among whom were Oskar Morawetz, Bruce Mather, and R. Murray Schafer. It should be pointed out that the relationship Gould had with Guerrero was not totally the traditional teacher-pupil rapport. Very often Guerrero treated Gould as an equal mind, exploring music together (Gould, 1983a).

Gould was also influenced by Artur Schnabel's musical approach. This attitude considers music as rooted in the imagination first, then gives it expression through various media. The physical embodiment of musical gesture is secondary to the unembodied musical idea. Gould, like Schnabel, viewed music as a private activity, not a public one. He believed one should avoid performance activity that is focused on displaying the performer as a virtuoso.

Gould practiced this attitude by favoring nonvirtuoso repertoire. He would often include works of Byrd, Gibbons, Sibelius, Anhalt, and Bach (easy ones) in recital programs and recordings. These works are not considered part of the pianist's virtuoso repertoire. Even though Gould was a great virtuoso he did not prefer composers whose work is traditionally considered part of a virtuoso's repertoire (e.g., Chopin and Liszt).

In addition, both Gould and Schnabel developed their musical ideas to a great extent away from the keyboard. They needed very little repetition in practice sessions in order to physically realize their musical ideas. As adults, both artists were able to absorb music away from the instrument without the need for long practice hours at the keyboard. In Gould's case this habit was developed as a child. Both artists considered themselves first musicians and then pianists. The piano was only a medium by which they could convey their analysis and conceptions of the music.

In February of 1944, Gould competed in the Kiwanis Music Festival and won the piano competition. Payzant (1978) wrote that although Gould was only eleven years old he ranked highest among several older advanced musicians. In 1945 he passed the professional level associateship examination in piano performance administered at the conservatory.

Gould also made a successful debut as organist in a Casavant Society concert at Eaton Auditorium on December 12, 1945. Robert Fulford (1983) wrote that people were greatly impressed and astonished by Gould, the child, who could play with such brilliant technique and interpretive intuition.

During the same year Gould began high school at the Malvern Collegiate Institute in a special program of studies which enabled him to devote much of his time to music study. Consequently, he ended his studies there without a diploma.

On May 8, 1946, Gould performed, for the first time, as piano soloist with the Toronto Conservatory Orchestra at Massey Hall at the conservatory. He played the first movement of Beethoven's *Fourth Piano Concerto in G Major*. Journalists write that Gould was a young prodigy worthy of further attention.

In June of that same year Gould passed the associateship exam in music theory. On October 28, 1946, at age fourteen, he was awarded the associate diploma from the Toronto Conservatory of Music.

Payzant (1978) noted that the year 1947 also marked a series of firsts for Gould. In January he gave his first performance with a professional orchestra of the complete Beethoven *Fourth Piano Concerto in G Major* with the Toronto Symphony Orchestra under the direction of Bernard Heinze. In April he played his first public solo recital at the Toronto Conservatory.

On October 20, 1947, he performed his first public piano recital as a professional artist. Walter Homburger, Gould's managing agent until 1967, presented the concert at Eaton Auditorium. John Beckwith wrote about Gould's rendition of the Beethoven *Piano Sonata, Opus 31, #2,*

> The central adagio movement is so full of silence in its opening theme that with most players one simply loses interest. Gould conveyed the feeling of forward-driving energy through the silences, so that their later filling-out with variational filigree came as an especially beautiful evolution. (Gould, 1983a, p. 66)

Gould was very busy during these high school years. In 1948 he composed his first piano sonata. He experimented with twelve-tone as well as other techniques. He also performed Sunday afternoon concerts at the Art Gallery of Toronto, network radio recitals for the Canadian Broadcasting Corporation (CBC), and continued to perform at the Toronto Conservatory of Music.

In 1951 he terminated his studies at the Malvern Collegiate Institute. He was a capable student, and it is clear that his interests in composition and performance were beyond what the school could offer him.

The following year Gould ended his formal piano studies with Alberto Guerrero. By the time he was twenty his musical accomplishments were many: he had performed with orchestra a dozen or more times, he had toured Canada as a solo artist, and he had performed over the CBC media.

After ending his piano studies with Guerrero, Gould retreated to his parents' cottage in Uptergrove, ninety miles north of Toronto. It was there that he spent the next few years working the piano and considering his future in music. Joseph Roddy (1983) wrote that Gould came to the conclusion, at that time, that the piano was too limited an instrument to express his musical ideas. What he really wanted to do was to become a composer. But he also realized that a career as a pianist would be much more practical for him.

Payzant (1978) pointed out that during this time of almost complete isolation, Gould presented a few concerts and broadcasts for the CBC. However, for the most part, he worked intensely to test whether he possessed the necessary attributes to be a world-class pianist. After this period of self-introspection he emerged on the threshold of his international career.

CAREER YEARS

Gould's 1955 American debut recital programs in Washington, D.C., and New York City, respectively, were highly original and bold in concept. Gould played music of the sixteenth-century composer Sweelinck; the late-Renaissance, Jacobean English composer Orlando Gibbons; five J. S. Bach Sinfonias; J. S. Bach's *Partita #5 in G Major;* the Berg *Piano Sonata, Opus 1;* Beethoven's *Piano Sonata, Opus 109;* and the Webern *Variations for Piano, Opus 27.* Concerning this program Richard Kostelanetz wrote, "Few pianists made such auspicious American debuts as Gould did in 1955, first in Washington and then at New York's Town Hall" (Gould, 1983a, p. 135).

The critical review for these recitals recounts that Gould was totally equipped as a technician and subordinated his virtuosity for the sake of expressiveness. His ability to clarify the music for the listener pleased his reviewers.

On January 12, 1955, the day following his New York debut recital, Columbia Records signed a long-term, exclusive contract with Gould. Walter Homburger, Gould's manager, said that it was the first time Columbia Records had offered a contract to an unknown artist solely on the merits of a debut recital (Payzant, 1978).

Gould's first project under the recording contract was Bach's *Goldberg Variations.* This was a work that was not performed in public, with the exception of performances by Rosalyn Tureck. The fact that Gould chose the *Goldberg Variations* as his first commercial recording exemplified his unique penchant for championing relatively unknown compositions. The recording was an immediate commercial and artistic success, and it helped project Gould among the world's foremost ranking contemporary pianists.

His second recording project with Columbia was the last three piano sonatas of Beethoven: Opus 109, Opus 110, and Opus 111. Like the *Goldberg Variations,* these works were usually performed by seasoned artists at the end rather than the beginning of their careers. Gould stood uniquely apart from the prevailing norm of other pianists.

In 1956, Gould published his most important composition, the *String Quartet, Opus 1.* Gould considered this late-romantic sounding piece an example of his early period writing. It was published by Barger and Barclay of New York City. In February of that same year it was

premiered by the Montreal String Quartet in a CBC
broadcast. Later it was premiered in the United States and
recorded by members of the Cleveland Orchestra.

In March of 1956 Gould performed Beethoven's *Piano
Concerto #4* with the Detroit Symphony under the baton of
Paul Paray. In January of 1957 Gould gave his first concert
with the New York Philharmonic with Leonard Bernstein
as conductor of Beethoven's *Piano Concerto #2*. This was
the beginning of Gould's association with Bernstein. Their
performing together ended in the infamous 1962 concert
of the Brahms *Piano Concerto in d minor*.

At that concert, Bernstein disavowed himself from the
extremely slow tempi on which Gould insisted. He an-
nounced on the stage, just prior to the performance, that
he did not agree with Gould's musical ideas but would go
along with them for the sake of musical experimentation,
since he greatly respected Gould's musical gifts and found
the notion of the whole experience interesting.

Of this event Bernstein wrote, "The result in the papers,
especially the *New York Times*, was that I had betrayed my
colleague. Little did they know—though I believe I did say
so to the audience—that I had done this with Glenn's
encouragement" (Bernstein, 1983, p. 19). A scandal
erupted and the critics had a heyday of maligning both
Bernstein and Gould, when in fact, this concert was
performed as a kind of intellectual experiment in musical
interpretation with consent from both artists.

Gould was the first North American pianist to perform
in the Soviet Union. In 1957, he played four concerts in
Moscow and four in Leningrad. The journalists record him
as a cultural ambassador who had enormously successful
reactions from the Russian people.

Joseph Roddy wrote that the Russians were as impressed
with Gould's Bach as they were with Van Cliburn's
Tchaikovsky. "After Gould played the 'Goldberg Variations' in Moscow's Tchaikovsky Hall, one critic concluded
that the only possible explanation for such excellence was
that the pianist must be more than two hundred years old
and an ex-pupil of Bach himself" (Roddy, 1983, p. 121).

While he was in Russia, Gould found time to lecture on

Berg and Schoenberg at the Moscow Conservatory. Some members of the audience showed their appreciation by giving him the complete piano works of Miaskovsky. However, some conservatory pedagogues walked out protesting Gould's Western ideas.

Gould's Berlin debut was in May 1957 when he performed Beethoven's *Piano Concerto #3 in c minor* with the Berlin Philharmonic conducted by Herbert von Karajan. Again Joseph Roddy recalled the performance: "H. H. Stuckenschmidt, Germany's most respected music critic, was moved to call Gould the greatest pianist since Ferruccio Busoni, the Italian-born virtuoso who made his reputation in Berlin in the early nineteen-hundreds as the greatest pianist since Franz Liszt" (Roddy, 1983, p. 121).

Additional highlights in Gould's concert career include a June performance, the last concert of his European tour of that year, in Vienna. He then returned to North America and continued to make recordings for Columbia Records and perform concert tours. In May of 1958, Gould played Beethoven's *Concerto #4* with the Philadelphia Orchestra under Eugene Ormandy. And in August he returned to Europe to perform the Bach *Concerto in d minor* at Salzburg.

The years from 1959 to 1964 were marked by increased activity in speaking about music rather than performing it. Gould lectured at the Gardner Museum in Boston, the University of Cincinnati, Hunter College in New York, the University of Wisconsin, Wellesley College, and the University of Toronto. Concerning the Hunter College lecture/recital, several members of the audience walked out when it became apparent that Gould would not be playing the piano much throughout the lecture. They envisioned Gould primarily as a pianist. The fact that he was interested in writing and giving lectures was dismissed as eccentric behavior not to be taken seriously by some critics. They felt Gould should confine his artistic and creative activity to the piano.

In 1963, the University of Toronto awarded Gould an honorary doctorate. Traditionally the musician who receives an honorary degree gives a musical performance at the ceremonies. Gould gave the convocation address. At that point in his career, he favored talking to playing in public (Payzant, 1978).

On March 28, 1964, Gould performed his last public recital in Orchestra Hall, Chicago, Illinois: Beethoven's *Piano Sonata Opus 110*, Krenek's *Third Piano Sonata*, Bach's *Partita #4 in D Major*, and fugues from Bach's *The Art of the Fugue*. He ended his public performing career in order to devote his energies exclusively to recording, film, radio, and writing projects.

RECORDING

The bulk of Gould's recorded performances are on the piano except J. S. Bach's *The Art of the Fugue*, Fugues 1–9 (organ), 1962; and G. F. Handel's *Suites 1–4* (harpsichord), 1972.

In January 1962, Fugues 1–9 of *The Art of the Fugue* were recorded on the Casavant Frères organ of All Saints Kingsway Anglican Church in Toronto. Gould and the technical crew ran out of recording time in Toronto and chose to record the incompleted portions in a theological college chapel in New York City.

The Casavant Frères organ at All Saints Church was a large instrument with a huge pedal division capable of baroque sounding registrations. Unfortunately, Gould did not plan his registrations to exploit this organ's full range of capabilities. Fuzzy registrations resulted. In addition, it appears that Gould rarely used the pedal in this recording.

Some critiques to this recording were negative. However, Payzant, comprehending Gould's intention of capturing Bach's didactic purposes for these pieces, wrote,

> Gould's album, *The Art of the Fugue*, Fugues 1–9, is not a showpiece; it is a set of essays—one essay about each of the first nine fugues, each in the form of an extremely original and revealing interpretation. Like every Gould recording it is a mine of fresh insights and novel perspectives. And it excels almost every other Gould recording in its exuberance. (Payzant, 1978, p. 101).

Gould's recording of Handel's *Suites 1–4* took place in the Spring of 1972. Robert P. Morgan wrote that Gould seemed to be completely at home with the harpsichord. Gould transferred "his phenomenal pianist technique to the new instrument" (Morgan, 1973, p. 84).

However, Gould commented that his harpsichord playing upset his piano playing (Gelatt, 1962). Payzant also wrote, "Gould's Handel record and his harpsichord broadcasts confirm that he does not accommodate to this [meaning harpsichord tactile requirements]; he slams the keys into their beds" (Payzant, 1978, p. 101).

That Gould could create the illusion that he was technically comfortable with the harpsichord is remarkable and a credit to his recording acumen. The fact that Gould produced only one harpsichord recording also supports the claim that he considered this instrument upsetting to his technique. He might have made other recordings if this were not the case.

Gould's discography cites over ninety recordings created from the 1950's until his death in 1982. For Gould, the recording studio was a place where he could make music in a much more personal, direct manner than the concert stage. He seems to consider that greater intimacy between the performer and listener was possible. He could phrase and temper the music as if communicating to individuals in close proximity rather than to large audiences in oversized auditoriums.

The positioning of the microphones as well as the final mixes opened up creative possibilities for him that could not exist in conventional performances. Gould's concert recitals taped for CBC Radio are examples of Gould's experimentation with microphone placement.

A different level of artistic creation was possible with an end result that might include the input of several people (i.e., the performer, the recording engineers, the producer, technicians, and others). For Gould, a recording was a cooperative event and the judgment of the performer no longer solely determined the musical result. Each person involved could potentially contribute to a single artistic vision.

The recording medium liberates the performer from consumer restraints by utilizing only repertoire that appeals to audience reaction. Since audience reaction is not an immediate, primary concern, the performer could possibly develop broader, more personally interesting repertoire.

In the safe, womb-like atmosphere of the recording studio, the artist can transcend the limited environment of a live performance. The imagination is free of performance constraints during post-taping reflection (Gould, 1966d).

Gould was not comfortable with the dynamic that very often exists between performer and audience. Public performance seems to be a kind of sport in which the blood-thirsty crowd is poised to prey upon the vulnerable artist-performer. Metaphors that are used to describe concert situations (e.g., "the performer must conquer his audience" or "the performer must be triumphant") illustrate that even in the language of the concert world a kind of competitive, sports-like spirit is pervasive (Gould, 1984b).

Audience applause tempts the performer to apply attention-grabbing tricks that, according to Gould, are perversions which detract from musical integrity. Technology could redeem the artist from these potentially dehumanizing effects of the crowd's dynamic. Payzant (1978) wrote that in Gould's eyes recording technology could take on moral proportions and save the artist from the horrors of live performance by intervening between culture and man's sinful beastliness. Through recording, the artist is no longer at the mercy of a group consciousness that could possibly influence the performer in a negative, less than authentic way.

The use of the recording media frees the artist to practice the ideas presented above and other notions of Gould's musical philosophy, for the recording studio is a medium comprised of "limitless possibilities" for the performer, listener, and composer (Payzant, 1978).

THE PERFORMER

One possibility for the performer, according to Gould, would be the ability to revise a work of performance by choosing selected recorded takes for the final product. This process, which Gould employed often, enables the performer to control the outcome of performance to a much higher degree than that of a live performance in a concert hall.

Gould abhorred the fact that in a live performance the performer had only one chance at artistic interpretation. Gould believed this restriction unnecessarily limited artistic expression. The recording studio freed one of "non-take-twoness," a term coined by Gould, and the artist could adjust and readjust an interpretation at will. One could have within one's grasp the resources to transform recorded sound. Consequently, this could generate new artistic ideas or simply overcome limitations posed by the instrument or acoustics (Gould, 1984b).

Gould stated that in performance one should strive for a rendition that clarifies the "backbone" or structure of a composition. He believed that one's approach should be spare and analytical, the microphone being the ideal medium for such an approach. Depending on its design and positioning, the microphone "hears" whatever it is programmed to hear. Its technology can bring the listener into a potentially greater awareness of the music's structure. It is superior to live performances in concert halls because of the inherent acoustical limitations in auditoriums.

Since the microphone "dissects and analyzes" the music, it inspires the performer to develop attitudes that are very different from those fostered in the spread out acoustic of the traditional concert hall. These attitudes foster clarity, acoustical dimension, and an illusion of closeness. Gould thought that these attitudes, inculcated through the recording medium, were superior for achieving musical understanding in both the performer and listener.

Gould went a step further in predicting that the recording medium would transform performers' approaches to performance (Gould, 1966d). The performer who records could possibly develop a broader base of repertoire and be free to experiment with repertoire that did not have immediate audience appeal. After completing a recording project the performer is free to leave it and go on to other projects. He could explore music from stylistic periods that are not commonly performed in live concerts.

The performer could investigate a wide selection of repertoire to determine which compositions were more acoustically suitable for concert performances (Gould, 1966d). (Recording the complete works of a particular composer would be an example of the enormous scope of these productions.) This in turn could lead to an archival approach to recording.

Gould thought recordings could preserve the composer's authoritative performances of their works. (This, indeed, is a popular practice in today's recording industry.) The following are some positive and negative effects Gould (1966d) prognosticated for such a practice:

Negative Effects: (1)   It would limit or constrain other interpretations of the works. (2)   Our expectations that live performances must be like the near-perfect recorded performances will weaken concert attendance.

Positive Effects: (1)   Composers could possibly become better performers because their performing skills would be in greater demand. (2)   In developing these archival recordings the musicologist, and not the performer, will be the key figure in the discovery and realization of untapped repertoire. (3)   Perhaps the performer will also turn quasi musicologist in the Gouldian expansion of his musical roles.

The roles traditionally separate in music are potentially fused when working with the recording medium. The performer could conceivably act as musicologist and composer-recreator. Additionally, because of the inherent archival dimension in recording, the performer can potentially establish a relationship with a work very much like the composer's connection (Gould, 1966d).

Gould speculated that the amalgamation of the technician and performer roles could produce an interesting effect. A new species, the technician-become-performer, could evolve in the editorial afterthought of performance. Under this new rubric, attention to technical detail in capturing the composer's intent will be just as important as the performer's traditional rendition of a work (Gould, 1966d). It is clear that the performer must gain technical skill in recording in order to have meaningful input.

To support the claim that the technology of the microphone and other aspects of recording do not necessarily detract from the music but could potentially add value to it, Gould conducted an experiment.

A group of professional musicians, technicians, and laymen were selected as subjects. The subjects were tested to determine if they could detect the splices in a recorded passage. The outcome of this loosely controlled experiment showed that the subjects could not hear where the splices occurred in a recording (Gould, 1975f).

This reinforced Gould's practice of many splices when he recorded standard repertoire as well as his original radio compositions. The listener could not hear the splices and, therefore, the quality of the performance was not compromised. The end justified the technical means. Gould strongly believed that post-taping afterthought was invaluable because it could free the imagination from limitations inherent to the live performance experience (Gould, 1966d).

THE LISTENER

Gould recognized in recording technology the opportunity for multiple hearings of a single performance. The listener cannot only listen at will to a recording but also stop the recording when desired and repeat a particular passage. Thus, the listener has the opportunity for acquiring a deeper awareness of the inner workings of the music. The listener possesses all the time necessary to establish greater intimacy with the work. The listener is put in a position to potentially penetrate the various levels of understanding necessary to more fully comprehend the significance of a work.

Since a live performance cannot stop or repeat itself, it is possible with recording technology to perceive more than the generalities of panoramic vistas often presented in such performances. In recording, the listener can possibly capture the detail lost in a performance that steams ahead.

Another insight Gould made concerning recordings is the listener's potential power to make artistic decisions and control the immediate outcome of a recording. Through the technology that was available during Gould's lifetime the listener was already capable of easily adjusting volume, balance, tempo, tonal quality, clarity, and stereo or monaural sound of a recording. This made it possible for the listener to become more of a participant in the musical experience. Gould felt that recording technology's capability for listener intervention was its greatest achievement. The future of music as an art would be profoundly impacted because the listener could become potentially active, rather than passive, in the listening experience (Gould, 1966d).

Gould further predicted that the future listener's role would be more like the composer-performer. The listener of the future could purchase recording-kits which would consist of several different performed versions of a particular composition. These readings could be performed by one or several different artists. By using splicing techniques the listener could choose and reassemble whichever versions or takes that embodied the desired interpretation. At another time, the "listener turned quasi composer-performer" could change the previous interpretation by again rearranging the materials provided in the kit.

This process is very much like the process Gould used in creating his own recordings. After making several takes of selected passages of a composition, Gould would decide which takes best served his interpretive vision of the work. This process occurred either immediately after recording or at some future date. The time sequence meant little to Gould.

Gould believed that by distancing himself from the interpretation of the moment he could permit the work to open up new insights for keener artistic understanding that might be missed on initial performance.

Gould greatly valued the recording process in that, through it, he could achieve solitude, and yet, be intimate with the listener in ways not available in live concert hall performances. He could connect with the listener on auditory and intellectual planes. Payzant (1978) pointed out that the recording system which physically separated Gould from the listener also welded him to the listener. The kind of immediacy gained through recording processes appealed to Gould who tried in his musical projections to strip away any distracting phenomena (e.g., the visual aspects).

Gould saw in recording the potential for creating sounds possessed of characteristics which were not available to previous generations. These traits would include greater analytic clarity, more immediacy, and almost a sense of tactile immediacy (Gould, 1966d).

THE COMPOSER

Recording techniques presented not only new creative opportunities for the composer working in this medium but also influenced conventional compositional procedures. Gould proposed that recordings influenced composers both directly and indirectly, if not subliminally (Gould, 1966d).

Recording techniques have evolved in a manner similar to the evolution of occidental music. Conventional musical forms and procedures have traced a path from the relatively simple to the more complex and sophisticated. Likewise, recording techniques have passed from primitive sound reproduction to sound manipulation limited only by the development of the technology.

The following are some of the capabilities of recording technology: (a) sound parameters like frequency and amplitude can be altered through frequency and amplitude modulation; (b) the sound's shapes and timbres can be altered through splicing; (c) the sound's attack and release can be transformed, eliminated, shortened, or lengthened.

With the development of binaural, multitrack recording procedures, the illusion of the sound source moving back and forth from speaker to speaker, known as panning, is possible. Sounds can be located according to speaker placement, and the change in reverberation characteristics can simulate changes in the perception of depth. Clearly, the possibilities are vast in the combinations and alterations effected upon sound.

Gould wrote that the methods used for sound manipulation found in recording technology have easily transferred to conventional compositional idioms. Gould cited the following as examples of this phenomenon: the repeated note pattern, with measured crescendo and diminuendo; the relationship between close-up and distant musical ideas; the quasi-mechanical ritardando or accelerando; and finally the controlled release and attack sound. These processes have been borrowed by the post-Western idioms that have influenced modern compositional practice (Gould, 1966d).

Gould used the work of Arnold Schoenberg, whom he considered the twentieth century's leading musical radical, to illustrate the significance of the recording phenomena on the composing process. He wrote that it is difficult to think about Schoenberg's opus, especially his earlier work (e.g., Serenade, Opus 24, or the Septet, Opus 29) without recognizing the connection between instrumental combinations and mobile microphone dissection (Gould, 1966d).

Gould (1966d) made a further observation in the fact that many composers create in their works today apparent balances that are unobtainable in the concert hall. The contemporary composer has absorbed features of the recording gesture that have changed his ways of hearing and creating. Electronic devices have inspired changes in conventional musical gesture and modes of compositional expression have evolved to include the following: multimedia presentations; spatial, rhythmic, and dynamic modulation; Doppler effects; mixed and intermedia; antimusic (benign and dangerous sounds); pointillism; and *klangfarbenmelodien*.

Recording's impact on composers has also taken away

the privileged autocracy in which composers have functioned exclusively in the past. The new composer very
often involves others in the decision-making processes, and
indeed, the separate roles of composer, technician, and
performer are more readily fused because of recording's
impact on music (Gould, 1966d).

Another advantage for the composer is the archival
aspects of recording mentioned earlier. Gould felt that our
musico-historical perspective of non-Western music was
myopic. The archival aspects of recording, which Gould
considered a vehicle for reflection, facilitated "the acceptance of a multi-faceted chronological concept" of music
history and aesthetics. Gould believed that these recordings promoted a more tolerant acceptance of the artistic
by-products of cultures that are not contained with the
narrow parameters of Western historical chronology. This
could in turn promote a cross-cultural diffusion of compositional style and nonconformist historical attitudes (Gould,
1966d).

CONCLUSIONS ON RECORDING

From his very first disc Gould employed his original
philosophy of recording. The recording process was not a
continuous event preserved on tape but rather a series of
takes in which Gould decided at another time which ones
would be used for the recording's final release. The use of
this methodology, apparently, did not detract in any way
from the success of the final product.

Concerning the recording of the *Goldberg Variations*
Nathan Broder wrote, "Taken as a whole, this is an
extraordinary performance that leaves one eager to hear
what else this very gifted player can do" (Broder, 1956).
Roland Gelatt wrote that Gould's recording of the Goldberg Variations impressed most who heard it with its
brilliance and imagination. Gelatt declared that Gould's
originality cannot be denied (Gelatt, 1956).

As was cited earlier, this Bach recording catapulted
Gould into a major performing career as both recording
artist and stage performer. In spite of his unusual interpre-

tations and methods in recording, Gould's recordings usually met with positive, if not enthusiastic, approval from the public and critics. The sometimes maverick interpretations he had a penchant for were not treated as anomalies but as artistically prophetic and insightful. This brings to mind the following questions: Why did the public very often perceive Gould as an oracle and not an aberration, in spite of his, at times, eccentric behavior? And why did he apparently stand so apart from many world-class pianists?

Perhaps the answers to these questions hinge on the fact that Gould offered to the listener much more than conventional musical ideas. He experimented with how musical ideas would react, open up to, and interface with other ideas. He probed, and sometimes, even toyed with music, often revealing surprisingly fresh insight. He functioned very much like the jazz musician who holds improvisation to be the essence of musical process. His original interpretations both illuminated the structure of a composition as well as explored a rare depth of feeling. His highly original mode of execution, which was oftentimes called provocative and brilliant, implemented his life's philosophy.

Those who oppose Gould's methods and ideas level other questions to be addressed. These questions are concerned with the artistic integrity of his process. Is the artistic integrity of a composition preserved if its recording is produced by a series of separate "takes"?

Critics of Gould's methods claim that artistic integrity is compromised when the chronological sequence of performing parts of a composition is interrupted. They assert that splicing techniques destroy the inherent dramatic continuity and the ecstatic inspiration of a unified performance is lost.

The roles of the producers and technicians involved in the artistic decisions of a recording are also questioned. Those opposed to communal artistic decision making purport that the artist is supreme in artistic decisions and others should stay out of this process. While critics still champion the supremacy of the artist, the very nature of the recording phenomenon prohibits this. The responsibility of authorship must be divided among a number of relatively anonymous people in a very pre-Renaissance fashion. Each person has an expertise that the others rely on for the finished product.

Finally, Gould's rebuttal to all criticism leveled against altered recordings is rooted in the notion that recordings should not be compared with live performances. Each is an art to be valued separately. The artistic integrity of the art of recorded works emanates from the intrinsic nature of the recording process just as the live performance draws its power from its medium.

FILM

Gould's activity in film was varied. He participated as a performer, writer, producer, composer, and arranger. His films were produced either for the theater or television. For whatever reasons, public television in the United States has basically ignored these films even though they have been widely shown by the British Broadcasting Corporation, the Canadian Broadcasting Corporation, and even French Television.

As a performer Gould assumed the roles of soloist (*Goldberg Variations,* 1981, Bruno Monsaingeon, director, Clasart Films), chamber musician (*Duo—Glenn Gould with Yehudi Menuhin,* 1965, CBC), and lecture-recitalist (*Glenn Gould Plays Bach; A Question of Instruments,* 1981, Bruno Monsaingeon, Clasart Films).

Gould championed the concert film in which he was successful in producing visual and artistic products in that, in the words of television critic Jack Hiemenz, "we actually forget the television medium's inherent limitations" (Hiemenz, 1984). These were not the diversions of an amateur, but professional quality creations.

Gould performed piano background music for the following films: (1) *Slaughterhouse Five,* Universal Pictures, 1972, directed by George Roy Hill; (2) *Spheres,* National Film Board of Canada, 1969, directed by Norman McLaren and Rene Jodoin; (3) *The Terminal Man,* Warner

Brothers, 1974, directed by Michael Hodges. He was often
music director and carefully matched the music to fit the
dramatic event.

Gould served as composer or arranger in the following
films: (1) *Slaughterhouse Five,* Universal Pictures, 1972,
directed by George Roy Hill; (2) *So You Want to Write a
Fugue,* by Glenn Gould, 1974, directed by Bruno Monsaingeon for French television.

In the capacity of writer-producer, Gould produced a
number of films about musical topics that range from
commentary about Byrd and Gibbons to Webern. In a
truly contemporary approach, Gould often espoused controversial, radical opinions that were designed to shock and
provoke reaction in his audiences. The multitalented
Gould, who has been called a Renaissance man, expressed
his seemingly outrageous views in order to stimulate his
audience to think about art and its kaleidoscopic impressions and manifestations.

Areas of discussion included questions about the following: instrumentation in Bach's music; a documentary on
the development of Russian music; a documentary/recital
on Beethoven; a documentary on the life of the Canadian
north; Toronto; a documentary on the diversity of developments in music since World War II; music and technology; Strauss; Scriabin; Berg; Webern; radio as music; a
documentary on Glenn Gould.

The possibility of taping nonsequential events when
filming intrigued Gould as much in filmmaking as it did in
the recording process. He employed this technique freely.
A good example of this is the film *The Goldberg Variations.*

Even though the film *The Goldberg Variations* (Monsaingeon, 1981) appears to be the result of a continuous,
sequential taping it is not. It is the product of expert
editing. The film's takes were selectively reordered in
order to project Gould's and Monsaingeon's artistic imagination. But when we view it we experience the illusion that
it is the product of a chronological sequence.

In a telephone conversation Gould had with the editors
of *Clavier* magazine in 1982, he described this taping of *The
Goldberg Variations.* He wrote, "The camera was absolutely

welded to the piano, and the visual architecture grows with each succeeding variation" (Gould, 1982a, p. 8). The film mimics the architecture inherent in the music and is structured to reinforce the musical shapes and climaxes.

Gould further endorsed splicing and editing by declaring that "splicing doesn't damage lines. Good splices build good lines and it shouldn't much matter if one use a splice every two seconds or none for an hour so long as the result appears to be a coherent whole" (Gould, 1975a, p. 18). Gould considered editing and splicing creative cheating (Payzant, 1978, p. 121).

For Gould, the producer in filmmaking was not bound to follow the original source of inspiration or screenplay. Just as the microphone "comments" on what it hears in a recording, so too, the camera becomes a commentator on the action in a film.

Through the media, Gould, the musical missionary iconoclast, was able to express his visionary ideas about music and other topics to a very large audience. This audience was certainly wider than one could imagine in a university classroom. He was able to communicate his ideas with the notion of effecting change in the lives of those who listened.

Those who listened apparently feel that he succeeded. Harris Goldsmith, *High Fidelity* magazine music critic, wrote about Gould, "It is the rare artist who undertakes to change our collective way of thinking and the even rarer one who succeeds" (Goldsmith, 1983, p. 54).

RADIO

Gould grew up in the radio world of the 1930's and 1940's. The radio was a vehicle by which the outside world could come to remote areas relatively untouched by global events and shattering ideologies. One could listen to the radio while maintaining a sense of detached distance and isolation, safe and secure in one's familiar surroundings. The integrity of one's personal identity could be preserved because the radio, which involved only the ear and one's imagination, was not totally invasive.

When Gould traveled with his parents on weekends to their cottage of Uptergrove, they would listen to the music and drama programs on the radio (Payzant, 1978). The radio accounted for much of Gould's self-education during that period of his development. For Toronto, called "Toronto the Good" during that time, was puritanical and restrictive. One could not attend live concerts on Sundays (Gould, 1983a, p. 91). The radio took over by supplying concert broadcasts.

Gould was fascinated with the radio as a medium for music, documentaries, and dramas. He began writing radio scripts during the mid-1950's because he was disillusioned with the programs that were aired at that time. He referred to them as "linear" or predictable in their form and presentation.

This inspired Gould to write programs that satisfied his need for variety and dramatic effect. His programs possessed dramatic range achieved through several layers of concurrent sound activity. It could also be said that Gould's programs shared the dramatic aims of motion pictures.

Gould's first radio drama was entitled *Glenn Gould on Sports*. In it, he interviewed himself about sports and competition. In a manner that would become typical of Gould, he wrote the dialogues for each character, and then acted out each part himself. The roles included a kayak champion and a Canadian welterweight. Ever since his play-reading days in Toronto's Rosedale, Gould loved to invent and act out fictitious characters (Roberts, 1983). The principal message of this program is the "moral" advantages of technology, a subject he explored several times in his writings.

Gould maintained that these radio programs were his primary compositional activity (Hurwitz, 1983). In utilizing the radio as a medium for composition he was able to complete the compositional projects that were largely left undone when executed with more conventional methods and materials. Technology inspired him to reach inside himself to uncover new talents that would help to fulfill his compositional ambitions.

Gould applied musique concrète techniques to create what he termed "contrapuntal radio." Payzant wrote, "They belong to a genre of which he can be said to be the inventor and, thus far, the only practitioner" (Payzant, 1978, p. 128).

The process was fourfold: (1) Gould sought and procured sound sources (often spoken dialogue and environmental sounds); (2) He recorded these sound sources using different types of microphones (e.g., omnidirectional, cardioid); (3) Gould then manipulated these sounds through editing and tape splicing; and finally, (4) He composed his program frequently applying traditional techniques of music composition (e.g., contrapuntal procedures to technological ways, or sound on sound, sound with sound, tape loops).

The results were contrapuntal radio documentaries. Payzant wrote about these works, "With each new hearing one learns more of the rules of the piece, and allows it to reveal its many details, layer upon layer, as one would do with a fugue by J. S. Bach" (Payzant, 1978, p. 129). Gould was drawn to contrapuntal textures because they represented the richest mode of musical expression. Edward Said expressed a description of counterpoint that Gould probably would have supported: ". . . its sheer complexity and frequent gravity suggest a formidable refinement and finality of statement" (Said, 1983, p. 47). This suggestion of final things implies contrapuntal modes that connect to an eschatology.

Gould's radio programs dealt with several subjects. He interviewed a theologian about theological issues, questioned a surveyor about William James, an economist concerning pacifism, and a housewife about the art marketplace (Gould, 1974b). However, most of the Gould documentaries were about situations that explore the concept of isolation which could be viewed as part autobiographical.

In his radio documentary about Schoenberg, Gould created interviews with John Cage, Erich Leinsdorf, Denis Stevens, Henri-Louis de La Grange, and Ernst Krenek. He spliced the comments to sound as if the subjects were conversing. He then designed suitable background music.

During this entire process, he acted as producer, assistant engineer, and maestro.

In the *Idea of North* Gould interviewed five people who appear to be traveling northward on a train. Like Gould, each person sought solitude and was not intimidated by the isolation of the north. Again, Gould spliced the individual interviews to seem like dialogues. Gould then used counterpoint and other musical maneuvers (e.g., the background train sounds are a "basso continuo") throughout the composition. The musical elements helped to create structure in this composition. The contrapuntal scenes also test one's ability to simultaneously listen to multiple layers of conversation. But, just like the last fugue from Verdi's *Falstaff*, every word in these conversations cannot be perfectly audible (Gould, 1984b).

These radio tape collages helped Gould to develop a multifaceted career in radio. In fact, as John Roberts wrote, "Gould's CBC radio career was branching in several different directions simultaneously" (Roberts, 1983, p. 244). He did much of his work for the Ideas Unit of the CBC. The following is a list of the programs he developed. He created a series called "The Art of Glenn Gould" in which he served as commentator. "Music of To-Day" was a long series of programs on Schoenberg. The "Sunday Supplement" discussed the phenomenon of the synthesized recording *Switched-On Bach*. In "The Scene" Gould offered views on competitive sports, games, and the effects of technology in the arts. "Ars National" had a five-week run. In it Gould introduced the music of his choice, and talked about himself. Other programs included "CBC Wednesday Night," "CBC Thursday Music," "Mostly Music," and "Listen to the Music."

Gould attained such importance for Canadian radio that he was asked to head the Canadian Broadcasting Corporation (Gould, 1983a, p. 254). He declined this offer in order to continue a life of musical creation entrenched in technology and the use of environmental sound. Gould thought that the notion of music has forever become inextricably connected with all the sounds of the environment (Gould, 1969e). It is interesting to note that this attitude is similar to the notions about environmental sound held by R. Murray Schafer, another Canadian composer. In the *Tuning of the World,* R. Murray Schafer expounded a theory that the world is a macrocosmic musical composition (Schafer, 1977, p. 5). He also stated that these sounds are not just acoustical events but are symbolic and have referential meaning (Schafer, 1977, pp. 169–180).

3. OVERVIEW OF LEADING PHILOSOPHIES OF MUSIC

INTRODUCTION

The purpose of this survey is to provide a theoretical background by which Gould's ideas can be better analyzed and understood. It also provides a foundation for the understanding of the philosophy of music education, which in several instances has drawn its theory and practice from the philosophy of music.

The philosophy of music shares with the history of aesthetics an extraordinarily diverse and vital cluster of intellectual theories. How does one present in a meaningful way the multifarious ideas inherent to these prominent theories about music?

This author proposes that this can be done if (1) the notion of "the philosophy of music" is discussed and defined; (2) the unique, distinguishing characteristics from every theory are presented; (3) reoccurring problems and issues relevant to these theories are discussed; and finally, (4) metatheoretical methodology is employed that yields broad, fecund theoretical results.

THE PHILOSOPHY OF MUSIC

One can criticize a specific philosophy of music under diverse rubrics, and depending upon the critical points in focus, varied interpretations can emerge. For example, Dunsby (1983) wrote that Leonard B. Meyer's opinions about music could be described as "distributional semiotics of musical communication" (Dunsby, 1983, p. 36). Likewise, Meyer has been viewed as an analytic formalist who sees meaning as intrinsic to a work (Meyer, 1967). Meyer can also be thought of as a referentialist in that he has written that things acquire meaning (their full nature is disclosed) when they are connected to or point to something beyond themselves (Meyer, 1956).

Each critical method of regarding music yields different meanings and insights. It takes pieces of knowledge and views them in several different contexts. Disparate viewpoints struggle, surface, and ultimately influence musical thinking and practice. Frequently, it is impossible to draw an exact parallel between the philosophies point by point because the issues a particular philosophy addresses may be completely or relatively ignored by the compared theory. For example, formalism does not invest as much weight in an investigation of emotion in music as does expressionism; nor does formalism explore the social significance of music like Marxist aesthetics. Each theory sees music through different critical lenses.

At first glance the literature appears to present a confusing situation. Even the vocabulary employed lacks uniformity (e.g., the term "musical aesthetics," which often suggests limited application of musical meaning, is used interchangeably with the expression "a philosophy of music," which as a rule implies a broader interpretation of musical meaning). Upon further investigation the reader discovers a metatheoretical unity. The theories represent various approaches to enduring questions of the philosophy of music. In spite of the differences displayed by the various philosophies there emerges a kind of gestalt of common recurrent problems of knowing and meaning.

A philosophy of music is not expected to offer absolute answers to all the problems inherent to understanding music. Rather, it is a continual exploration, a clarification, that examines problems. It is an ongoing process that should be marked by the use of critical analysis and the framing of questions about music (Rowell, 1983). Since the basic assumptions of a viable philosophical system determine to a degree the problems, all assumptions upon which it is based should be examined (Ferrara, 1978).

No philosophy appears from a vacuum. There are approaches and influences that reflect life interpretations. Each philosopher brings to philosophy a source of values about the world that ultimately contributes to philosophy. Philosophy is not just an analysis of ideas. It is also an expression of basic life choices and life interpretations.

The philosophy of music is not readily defined. This is true because thinkers do not freely agree as to what areas should be included in the domain of the philosophy of music. Some philosophers have discussed music in a limited way implying that meaning abides only in music's intrinsic dynamics. There is no mention of the broader issues and implications that could involve music. Most notable proponents of this viewpoint include Gurney, Hanslick, Stravinsky, and Hindemith.

Others recognize music's influence to embrace wider philosophical considerations. Their approach is to grant music significance within the greater context of culture and society. Followers of this persuasion include Langer, Ferrara, Epperson, and Adorno.

Within these two broad divisions subtler groupings emerge representing a diversity of approaches to music. This has characterized the shaping of twentieth-century speculation about music. Clearly, an all-encompassing philosophy of music does not exist. Seldom is there a philosophy that is systematically complete, totally isolated and developed within itself. Rather, there exists an interplay, a reciprocal action, of several, oftentimes diametrically opposed, ideas.

THE THEORIES

FORMALISM

The formalist experiences art primarily in an intellectual way. Form in art is identified and appreciated for its own sake (Reimer, 1970). Formalists construct their own realities that are relativistic and pluralistic. The meaning and value of human existence is contextual and formal when absolutes, beliefs, and paradigms vanish (Meyer, 1967). The formalist view of music was initially advocated by Edward Hanslick (1854) and Edmund Gurney (1880). In order to understand the contemporary formalist position, it is expedient to briefly examine its roots in Hanslick and Gurney.

Hanslick (1957) was the first persuasive critic of Romanticism. He theorized that Schopenhaurian musical aesthetics (i.e., music as the direct result of feelings) is unmusical and below art. In a similar way, Sparshott professed that music becomes art only when the feeling it conveys is indeterminate. He noted that Romantics fail to understand that feeling in music exists only as a result of the import of the music's form (Sparshott, 1980).

Sparshott explained further, "Moreover, the forms of music, and hence its beauty also, are sui generis, rather than manifesting a spiritual life that (as the romantic supposed) resists any ultimate differentiation" (Sparshott, 1980, p. 128).

Hanslick (1957) contended in *The Beautiful in Music* that music can represent the dynamic properties or modes of mental acts (i.e., slowness, speed, weakness, strength). But because music does not express itself in discursive language it lacks definite emotional connotation. While Hanslick admitted that the aesthetic is basically an emotional event, he rejected the idea that the value of art should be based on the emotions (Portnoy, 1954).

Hanslick argued that the "beautiful" in music is specifically musical in nature. The essence of music is sound and motion. Music does not essentially point to, express, or symbolize any extrageneric meaning. Langer wrote that Hanslick rejected the basic premise of semiotic aesthetics in that "the semantic use of music, the representation of emotive life," is absent in Hanslick's theory (Langer, 1942, p. 182).

Hanslick considered music to be a self-contained art that consisted of nothing more than form and content. The intrinsic qualities of a composition are the basis by which one should judge a work. Based on this Portnoy (1954) called Hanslick a purist and objectivist in his aesthetics.

The concept that form is content was central to Hanslick's argument concerning musical meaning. This argument is often believed to be a paradox in that form is its own content. But, it is not a reductio ad absurdum because in the musical symbol there is unity of form and content (Dahlhaus, 1982).

In addition, Dahlhaus stated that Hanslick's statement that form and content are one does not trivialize music because form means "inner form." Dahlhaus wrote, "Since Hanslick conceives form as spirit and essence, he can say meaningfully and consistently that form is a 'content' appearing in the material of tones . . . " (Dahlhaus, 1982, p. 53). Dahlhaus further wrote, "not only that form is spirit's expression, spirit's form of utterance, but that form itself is spirit" (Dahlhaus, 1982, p. 53).

To summarize Hanslick's view one could say: (1) the beautiful in music is specifically musical in nature; (2) the essence of music is sound and motion; (3) music can be apprehended only for itself. Hanslick's view, that music cannot express anything nonmusical of importance, was the foundation for contemporary theorists (e.g., Schenker, Reti, and Hindemith).

Gurney (1880) offered a penetrating analysis of musical form. He extended the concept that "form in music is spirit" by stating that the essential function of music is to inform us of unknown things through objective forms.

Gurney viewed a composition as a musical organism in "ideal motion." Ideal motion means that the ideas in music are capable of multiple meanings (Epperson, 1967). Musical motion displays the "ideal" suggesting at times physical motion and pointing to what Langer called "virtual motion." Gurney wrote of this experience,

> . . . its perpetual production in us of an emotional excitement of a very intense kind, which yet cannot be defined under any known head of emotion. So far as it can be described, it seems like a fusion of strong emotions transfigured into a wholly new experience. (Gurney, 1880, p. 120)

Gurney made a distinction between the impressive and expressive in music. Impressive is what Langer referred to as "semblance." Semblance is much more than physical sound or "aesthetic surface." It is an illusion, a sheer appearance, a symbol of forms of feeling (Langer, 1953, p. 107).

Epperson wrote,

> . . . impressiveness is the symbolic attribute which makes it generally accessible to the human understanding; it is precisely the transcendence of the particular in space and time that gives the relative autonomy to the art object. (Epperson, 1967, p. 155)

In contrast, the expressive in music are those qualities, images, and feelings that are describable.

Igor Stravinsky (1947) implemented Hanslick's work in the twentieth century by contending that music is meaningless outside of its congeneric dynamics. Musical speculation is consequently narrow in scope. Paul Hindemith (1961) also espoused the idea that music does not refer to anything outside itself.

Sparshott (1980) stated that another example of pure formalism can be found in the work of Nelson Goodman. He wrote,

> Goodman gives the concept of notation a precision it never had before, and reveals with disconcerting clarity its implications for the ideal relation between score and performance. His system assumes that a score functions as a definition of what a work is, rather than as a set of instructions for making music. . . . (Sparshott, 1980, p. 130)

Edward Lippman (1977), a modified formalist, proposed that meaning in music inheres in the music itself with no external reference. However, he stated that because musical meaning is internally significant it does not mean that it is unconnected to other experiences. Lippman's formalism is catholic in that he extended musical discussion to include psychological and historical considerations.

He wrote, "The structures found in music are in fact of such variety and complexity as to suggest at once, even if they are taken purely as structures that their origin lies in the whole nexus of man's social-historical nature" (Lippman, 1977, p. 156).

The mathematical theory of information has been another approach towards formalism. Theorists like Meyer (1967) and Youngblood (1958) have attempted to explicate music in terms of information theory that is semiological in character.

SEMIOTIC APPROACHES

The semiotic approach to understanding music occurs when music is thought to be a sign of something else. Beardsley (1966) pointed out that Ogden and Richards, in *The Meaning of Meaning* (1923), evolved a distinction between different "language functions," and especially, between the "referential function," in which a word, as an example, becomes fully symbolic, and the "emotive function," in which it serves as a sign of the speaker's feelings (Beardsley, 1966, p. 343).

Beardsley wrote that Charles W. Morris "proposed the definition of semiosis as 'mediated taking account of'—a sign is anything by means of which we take account in any way of something else" (Beardsley, 1966, p. 353). Morris developed the iconic sign theory. He maintained that aesthetic signs differ from other iconic signification in that their iconic signification is of human regional qualities. Their designation is also what Morris called value property (Beardsley, 1966).

Bent added, "The kindred approaches of semiotics and structuralism both tend to reduce all kinds of non-linguistic social communication to the state of natural language, semiotics by treating all the ways in which human beings signal to each other . . . " (Bent, 1987, p. 58).

Dunsby (1983) offered an explanation of semiotics as "a discipline which seeks to explain meaning as a relational phenomenon" (Dunsby, 1983, p. 27). Dunsby further

wrote, "For semiotics music is a cultural or social phenomenon, definable only in terms of its value held in a culture
according to a quantitative, qualitative, and analytical
interplay" (Dunsby, 1983, p. 28).

Bent (1987) noted that musical semiotics "views music as
a stream of sounding elements governed by rules of
'distributions': that is, of ways in which the elements
associate with or complement or mutually exclude each
other. Its aim is to state these rules as 'adequately' as
possible for any given passage of music, or work or group
of works: to formulate, in other words, a syntax for the
music" (Bent, 1987, p. 96).

Wilson Coker (1972) presented a detailed, cogent iconic
theory of musical aesthetics that is grounded in semiotic
ideas, psychology, and philosophy. The terminology borrowed from logic and semiotics is used in order to add
conceptual tools to theoretical language and analysis. A
metalanguage is developed that describes the inner and
outer dynamics of music.

Coker elaborately described the minute gestural processes of music in the light of Pierce's typology (i.e., the
Piercean triangle of sign, object, and interpretant). Coker
demonstrated how iconic sign theory gestures interconnect
in a hierarchy of values, and thus, has created a paradigm
by which all musical gesture can be analyzed and apprehended.

Jean-Jacques Nattiez (1975) borrowed from linguistics
the tree-structure diagram as a mode of presentation for a
semiotics of music. Dunsby wrote of Nattiez's conclusions:
(1) Functional models in linguistics may be helpful to
understanding music's autonomous organizational factors;
(2) ". . . the phonological model relying on a specific theory
of double articulation may correspond with the specific
musical model which distinguishes between structure and
esthetically pertinent structure"; (3)Comparative musical
semiotics should employ every useful linguistic model; (4)
Linguistics provides analogies to music's dichotomy between structure and meaning (Dunsby, 1983, pp. 41–42).

Nattiez in *Fondements d'une sémiologie de la musique* (1975)
developed a tripartitional model of musical activity that

includes *(a)* poetic—factors of creation in music; *(b)*
esthesic—factors of its reception; *(c)* neutral—a collection
of possible schemes of which the poetic and/or esthesic
"pertinence will be given later" (Dunsby, 1983, pp. 30–31).

However, Nattiez is removed from the position that
musical meaning contains a syntax. Dunsby further wrote,
"The lesson of Nattiez is that analysis can identify only the
multiplicity of forms or organization in a piece; it cannot in
itself reveal that a system, a unity, is at work" (Dunsby,
1983, pp. 37–38).

Clark (1982) instructed that semiotics sees music as an
ordering of symbols; ". . . if music has meaning, it must
mean something, namely whatever it is significant of, i.e.,
it's 'signified' " (Clark, 1982, p. 196). She also wrote of
Chomsky and his belief that music is identical to the natural
languages as a symbol system and can be analyzed,
contrary to Nattiez's position, in formal syntactical ways
(Clark, 1982, pp. 198–199).

Gardner (1982) declared, "Chomsky's lifelong pursuit
has been to understand the core of human language—the
syntax that undergirds our verbal output" (Gardner, 1982,
p. 19). Leonard Bernstein (1976) as well as Fred Lerdahl
and Ray Jackendoff (1983) have taken an interest in
Chomsky's theory in their work.

Susanne K. Langer's Theory of Presentational Symbolism

The work of Susanne K. Langer has stimulated much
interest and speculation in the last forty years. Few writers
of the philosophy of music have been as influential as S. K.
Langer (Hoaglund, 1980).

Langer's thought was strongly influenced by Cassirer's
theory of symbolism, German idealists (e.g., Kant,
Schopenhauer, and Schiller), and Gestalt psychologists.
Her ideas were also in congruence with Hanslick's formalist views in the sense that music possesses no literal
representational function. She departed from pure formalism in that she argued that music reveals emotional

forms that mediate truth in a different way than discursive language (Langer, 1942).

How does music accrue meaning? Langer answered this question by using music as a paradigm for a symbol system that is presentational rather than discursive (Sparshott, 1980). Langer demonstrated that music is capable of imparting its own semantic which is nondiscursive. Langer refuted literal assigned connotations, musical programs, and immutable values (Schwadron, 1967). Because music is devoid of fixed connotations, it does not necessarily follow that music possesses no meanings (the pure formalist position) or just random associations (Santayana's expressionism).

In explanation of Langer's theory Blum wrote, ". . . application of the Gestalt theory of isomorphism to music is introduced to explain how music can convey connotations which are neither assigned nor fortuitous" (Blum, 1959, p. 368). Through the absence of fixed meanings music can ideally transcend discursive language. The unique symbolism of the arts, while not exempt from logical treatment, is presentational in character (i.e., the meaning of the symbolic elements depends upon the meaning of the whole).

For Langer, the meaning of music is a philosophical problem requiring a logical study into the artistic and positivistic contexts. Langer's aesthetics reacted negatively to positivistic and behavioristic tendencies in philosophy and psychology. She held that these ideologies inadequately account for music by equating musical experience with the direct expression of actual emotions (Langer, 1942). Langer's philosophical contribution can gain much perspective if considered in the light of the positivistic-behavioristic, idealist-Gestalt controversies.

There are no works in our usual language sense to convey the full import or meaning of artistic expression. Yet, in spite of the lack of ordinary language, the arts do fall within a milieu that is reasonable and rational. This rationality is not conceived through discursive language (Langer, 1953). Rather, it enjoys its own dynamic symbolism that encompasses, among other elements, emotion and intuition. Art manifests the artist's intuition in the logic of the art work. Wade added, "Langer finds the principle of intuition at work in the ways of knowing and in the perception of works of art" (Wade, 1965, p. 174).

Langer agreed with Creighton that the rationality of art is also essentially cognitive and necessary (Langer, 1953). She rescues art from irrationality, chaos, supernaturalism, or whatever interpretation that reduces art to a subordinate position on the scale of human experience. She achieved this by arguing that humans' need for symbolization is primary, and by demonstrating that art, particularly music, fulfills this need to symbolize. Music is furthest removed from natural models in that it does not use language and functions from sound forms.

In Langer's examination of the four modes in the study of actual symbolism (language, ritual, myth, and music), music assumes an important position. She concluded, "The most highly developed type of such purely connotational semantic is music" (Langer, 1953, p. 101). Music, as other art, is about feelings but not from feelings.

Langer's teleological assumption states that because humanity has an inherent need to symbolize, people are symbol-making animals (Langer, 1942). According to Langer's teleological premise, music uniquely serves this symbol-making function.

LANGER AND EMOTIONS

Langer did not interpret music as if it were pure forms as did Hanslick and Gurney, but instead fused formalism to expressionism by attributing semantic import. Blum further explained, "Music symbolizes the emotions, not by virtue of chance subjective associations or assigned connotations, but by virtue of the formal analogy between music and the emotions" (Blum, 1959, p. 353).

How does music serve its symbolic function? Music

provides the symbolic formulation of knowledge about the emotions based on the epistemological assumption that all knowledge rests upon intuition. Music, as an expressive form, reveals aspects of the emotional life by means of "virtual time."

Langer drew on Henri Bergson's work (i.e., *Time and Free Will* [1889], *An Introduction to Metaphysics* [1903], *Creative Evolution* [1907], *Matter and Memory* [1897]) to develop her notion of multidimensional, qualitative, intuitively known musical time. This contrasts with time perceived as linear, qualitative, and cognitive.

Langer denied music any utilitarian value since its unique modus is illusory time and it is created only for aesthetic perception (Langer, 1942). She instead emphasized the expressive function of music.

Music is nonrepresentative. It does not, according to Langer, have literal context like a fact or a specific program attached to it. Langer explained that music is not self-expression, but "formulation and representation of emotions, moods, mental tensions and resolutions—a 'logical picture' of sentient, responsive life, a source of insight, not a plea for sympathy" (Langer, 1942, p. 222). The feelings in the music have a psychical distance involving insight and not direct emotional communication.

Langer shattered the notion that music expresses a composer's emotions. She claimed that if it were the function for music to express the composer's emotions then music history should demonstrate this kind of expressiveness in twentieth-century music. The fact that it does not is reflected in modern music's increasingly controlled forms. In Langerian terms, music possesses importance only when its symptomatic processes yield to symbolic functions (Blum, 1959, pp. 139–140).

The expressionist theory was rejected by Langer in the sense that she did not search for what an art work can mean but how the art work can possess meaning. Ferrara explained, "She presented a model to understand formally how it is possible for musical meaning to happen, not actually as it happens" (Ferrara, 1978, p. 22).

The musical art work achieves musical import by symbolizing the morphology of feeling. Music symbolizes the
morphology of feeling by virtue of the isomorphism
between the musical symbol and the life of sentience. It
does not yield knowledge of the physical world, or
metaphysical or mystical realms. It conveys that particular
knowledge called artistic insight that reveals objective
emotions analogically. Music exhibits nuances beyond and
above limited discursive symbols (Langer, 1953).

Leonard B. Meyer's Philosophy of Music

Leonard B. Meyer's philosophy of music is complex and is
not easily summarized. He has characterized himself as an
analytical formalist (1967). Yet, as was stated earlier,
Meyer's use of information theory is semiological in
character. His aesthetic philosophy is influenced by the
philosophical work of Dewey, Aiken, Langer, and Mead,
with the psychological models of Koffka, MacCurdy, and
Mursell (Schantz, 1983).

Meyer, as formalist, did not deal with ontological value
in a musical work. The relationship of a composition to the
world is circumvented. The composition's value is princi-
pally related to its grammatical simplicity. The syntactical
relationships in the composition are intrinsic to the work,
and thus, are unrelated to meaning in its traditional
(referential) sense (Ferrara, 1978).

MEYER AND MUSICAL MEANING

Meyer presumed the existence of musical meaning and
tried to clarify it. He wrote that things acquire meaning
when they are connected to or point to something beyond
themselves. In this way, the nature of a thing is disclosed
through this connection (Meyer, 1956). For Meyer, musical
meaning rests in the triadic relationship of stimulus, object,
and observer. Serafine (1980) called this implicative relationships.

EMBODIED MEANING AND REFERENTIAL MEANING

Meyer distinguished between embodied (absolute) meaning and referential meaning by offering the following explanations. *Embodied meaning* is the product of expectation. One musical event possesses meaning because it points to and causes us to expect another musical event. Meyer added that, "Because expectation is largely a product of stylistic experience, music in a style with which we are totally unfamiliar is meaningless" (Meyer, 1956, p. 35). He qualified this by stating that the music in the absence of embodied meaning may possess designative (referential) meaning.

For Meyer, embodied meaning means syntactical relationships within the music (Meyer, 1967). He enumerated three types of probability-based meanings within syntactical relationships in music: (1) hypothetical meaning—those that arise during the act of expectation; (2) evident meaning—when the relationship between the antecedent and its actual consequent is perceived; (3) determinate meaning—when all the meanings that the stimulus has had in the particular experience are realized and their relationships to one another comprehended as fully as possible (Meyer, 1956).

Hierarchical architectonic levels arise as these syntactical relationships operate. Meyer (1956) stressed that the various architectonic levels are interdependent and one should not emphasize one level at the expense of the others.

Referential meaning (designative) means the interaction between the musical symbol and the extramusical idea which it points to. Meyer (1956) explained his theory of referential meaning in music by creating three subdivisions: (1) image processes; (2) connotations; (3) mood responses.

An *image process* is the product of the connection between musical stimulus and extramusical experience. Meyer wrote, "These imaginings, whether conscious or unconscious, are the stimuli to which the affective response is really made" (Meyer, 1956, p. 256). Meyer divided image processes into two categories: (1) private image processes; and (2) collective image processes. Private image processes can be either conscious or unconscious. They are problematic because of the difficulty in following the relationship between the image processes and the musical stimuli. Collective image processes are common to an entire group of people within a culture.

Connotations are associations that are commonly experienced by a group within their culture. Meyer (1956) informed the reader there exist two kinds of connotations: (1) connotation by contiguity; and (2) connotation by similarity between the music and other types of experience.

Connotations by contiguity are those common associations music can assume that refer to referential images (e.g., the pipe organ is commonly associated with a church scenario; the gong often evokes thoughts of Oriental culture). These associations are not fixed but change with cultural changes.

Connotations by similarity concern similarities between music and other types of experience. Meyer wrote, ". . . it enables music to express what might be called the disembodied essence of myth, the essence of experiences which are central to and vital in human existence" (Meyer, 1956, p. 265). He further wrote, "Music presents a generic event, a 'connotative complex,' which then becomes particularized in the experience of the individual listener" (Meyer, 1956, p. 265). One associates musical ideas with qualities of other modes of perception. And thus, music and life are experienced in a dynamic process.

Schantz (1983) criticized Meyer's analysis of connotation by similarity because it implies referential meaning arises solely from the similarities that may occur between music and other experience modes. Schantz reasoned,

> Similarity does not necessarily indicate a cause-and-effect relationship and even if it does it does not show the direction of that relationship. Referential meaning, a cause-and-effect relationship, does occur in contiguous association but does *not* occur in "connotations" by similarity. (Schantz, 1983, p. 38)

Music may evoke *mood responses* on the part of the listener. Meyer noted that the moods connected with music are not spontaneous emotional reactions but stereotypical or designative emotional behavior. In addition, different musical devices (i.e., rhythmic, harmonic, and melodic configurations) become ". . . formulas which indicate a culturally codified mood or sentiment" (Meyer, 1956, p. 267).

Ferrara (1978) claimed that Meyer has not gone far enough in explicating the referential export in music. He stated that Meyer intellectualizes the mental processes of musical events rather than describes and probes musical import. Ferrara asserted that Meyer's attempt to go from syntax to axiology is a specious attempt at finding musical value and meaning. What is lacking is an ontological discussion of the "world" of the work.

MEYER AND MUSICAL STYLE

Musical styles, which embody syntactical relationships, are systems of sound relationships commonly accepted by a group (Meyer, 1956). They are "internalized probability systems" (Meyer, 1967, p. 8). The practical habits needed to respond to a particular musical style vary from culture and era. All traditional musical styles possess two common features: (1) syntactical relationship, and (2) the stable octave, fifth, and fourth as focal tones of the other tones of the system (Meyer, 1956).

Musical styles undergo continuous change. Meyer wrote, "As we listen to music we are constantly revising our opinions of what has happened in the light of present events" (Meyer, 1956, p. 49). This is significant because we are perpetually changing our expectations. Although repetition may be physically present, it never exists psychologically.

In his early work Meyer related his theory of musical style to information theory. He contended that deviation and uncertainty, which give music greater syntactical meaning (information), are similar to the psychostylistic conditions that express information (Meyer, 1967).

Meyer's theory uses information theory and other concepts of formalism to clarify musical meaning.

In a personal communication with Allen Schantz (1983), Meyer stated that he changed his position about deviation and uncertainty in that they do not yield greater meaning but new meaning in music. Deviation yields music a contemplative character. In this later position, Meyer viewed information theory with limited value and attested that stylistic value is related to richness rather than complexity.

Meyer expanded his idea called style deviation (complexity) to incorporate relational richness. He wrote,

> Relational results must, then, be distinguished from material means. When this is done, it is evident that what is essential in the evaluation of music are not the foreground (note-to-note) successions of pitches, durations, harmonies, and other musical parameters but the higher-order patterns created by these palpable means. What is crucial is relational richness, and such richness (or complexity) is in no way incompatible with simplicity of musical vocabulary and grammar. (Meyer, 1975–1976, pp. 693–694)

MEYER AND EMOTIONS

In a discussion of Meyer's book *Emotion and Meaning in Music* (1956) Schwadron explained,

> The central thesis of Meyer's psychological study are that emotion or affect is aroused when a tendency to respond is arrested or inhibited, and that emotional behavior is largely a learned cultural phenomenon rather than a natural one. (Schwadron, 1967, p. 39)

Meyer (1956) attempted to demonstrate how music's syntactical relationships bring forth emotion. It is based in part on MacCurdy's psychological theory of emotions. The theory claims that emotion or affect is stimulated when response is stopped or blocked. This idea is a direct outgrowth of Dewey's conflict theory of emotion, but stresses the stopping rather than the conflict of tendencies as the cause of emotions. In Meyer's theory of the relation of musical stimuli to emotional response, musical meaning occurs when expected responses to the music are delayed or blocked.

Meyer noted three significant differences between musical and nonmusical affective experience: (1) Musical stimuli are nonreferential; (2) In nonmusical experience, "tensions created by the inhibition of tendencies often go unresolved," and "In art, inhibition of tendency becomes meaningful because the relationship between the tendency and its necessary resolution is made explicit and apparent. Tendencies do not simply cease to exist: they are resolved"; (3) In nonmusical experience, "factors which keep a tendency from reaching completion may be different in kind from those which activated the tendency in the first place. . . . In music, . . . the same stimulus, the music, activates tendencies, inhibits them, and provides meaningful and relevant resolutions" (Meyer, 1956, p. 23).

Meyer applied this general theory of emotions to musical syntax. He sought to relate syntax to expressive meaning. His lack of representational meaning weakened his argument (Ferrara, 1978).

MEYER AND MORALITY

The later Meyer rejected the idea that music can improve morality or humanize. He utilized as an example the fact that although Germans were knowledgeable and devoted to musical greats of their culture (e.g., Bach and Beethoven), it did not prevent the atrocities of Nazi Germany. Meyer believed that the arts are not for something but are relevant to someone. They entertain ideas to pattern and structure the world (Meyer, 1979, pp. 136–137).

The early Meyer's vision of value is rooted in syntactical meaning and music's expressive meaning that allows the extra-aesthetic to be a means to maturity. Schantz wrote, "Self-realization becomes the ultimate goal of man's existence. Meyer's conclusions lead to a contemplative view of art and sow the seeds for disregarding ordinary experience as the content of art" (Schantz, 1983, p. 83).

In conclusion, Meyer wrote, ". . . in contending that the ultimate value of art lies in its ability to individualize the self, I am conscious of my opposition to those who, like Plato, Tolstoy, and the Marxists, would make aesthetic value a part of moral value" (Meyer, 1967, p. 40).

MEYER AND MUSICAL GREATNESS

Meyer (1967) argued that greatness in music transcends syntax and unites syntax to associative aspects of music. Greatness is related to the concept of the sublime. He concluded,

> These ultimate uncertainties and at the same time ultimate realities—of which great music makes us aware—result not from syntactical relationships alone, but from the interaction of these with the associative aspect of music. This interaction, at once shaping and characterizing musical experience, gives rise to a profound wonderment—tender yet awful—at the mystery of existence. And in the very act of sensing this mystery, we attain a new level of consciousness, of individualization. The nature of uncertainty too has changed. It has become a means to an end rather than an end to be suffered. (Meyer, 1967, p. 38)

Meyer ventured from the aesthetic to the metaphysical. He wrote,

> It is clear then that our hypothesis on the relationship of resistance and uncertainty to value transcends the realm of aesthetics. For the choice to be made, the question to be asked, is in the final analysis metaphysical. It is this: What is the meaning and purpose of man's existence? And though one's answer can be rationalized and explained— though one can assert that it is through self-realization that man becomes differentiated from the beasts—it cannot be proved. Like an axiom, it must be self-evident. (Meyer, 1967, p. 40)

EXPRESSIONISM

WHAT DOES MUSIC EXPRESS?

According to the expressionist theory, composers express their actual emotions in their music. Their psychological state arouses a musical reaction just as a blow to the finger stimulates cries of pain. A large number of music philosophers, critics, and musicians, particularly nineteenth-century German Romanticists, adopted this position.

The apex of this philosophical theory exists in the modern analytic school of thought, especially in logical positivists like Carnap and Wittgenstein (Blum, 1959). This position was also advocated by Benedetto Croce (1970) and R. G. Collingwood (1933).

Croce viewed aesthetics as the pursuit of intuitive knowledge. When impressions become clarified then they become intuitions. His formula, intuition = expression, became the prototype and influenced certain expressionist theories (Ferrara, 1978).

Beardsley wrote that for Croce,

> An artistic expression is always a complex, whose constituent expressions correspond to individual intuitions; but it has a unity of its own, that makes it a single expression which therefore must correspond to (or be identical to) a single intuition. (Beardsley, 1966, p. 322)

Croce thought that all people are artists in that they possess images; there is no separation of art from the rest of spiritual life; and fine art is just the most highly developed form of intuitive expression, just as science is the most highly developed form of logical knowledge. For Croce there is no separation of intuition from expression. And, the genuine work of art rests in the artist's mind. Croce's philosophy of mind is a metaphysics, a form of idealism, and his aesthetics is an essential part of it (Beardsley, 1966).

Collingwood, Croce's most widely studied and highly

regarded follower, clarified and expanded Croce's aesthetic theory. He charted a distinction between "mere" and
"true" expressions of feeling. Mere expression of feeling
conveys an idealized, virtual "feeling form," as opposed to
true expression of feeling, which is the product of the
composer's emotional experience and the expression of
those feelings through the composition (Ferrara, 1978).

WHAT DO WE MEAN BY THE STATEMENT "MUSIC EXPRESSES EMOTION"?

When we say that music expresses emotion (e.g., melancholy) we mean that music possesses an expressive property, not to be confused with the emotional state (e.g.,
melancholy), which we also possess as a certain emotional
state of being. The idea that music expresses emotion can
also mean that it affects the person in a certain way, either
by hearing the emotion in the music, or by feeling the
emotion as a result of the music (Stecker, 1984).

WHAT KIND OF EMOTION IS EXPRESSED IN MUSIC?

Stecker (1984) asserted that it is not necessarily true that
music consists of emotion just because we can be moved by
it. Rather, nonexpressive properties, (i.e., tempo, dynamics, harmony, melody) ambiguously symbolize emotional
states. He claims that hearing emotion in music is a
quasi-perceptual, quasi-imaginative activity.
    Hoaglund (1980) offered an alternative view. He argued
that art can possess expressible states that have intentional
objects. He also maintained that perhaps the expressive
power of instrumental music may derive from imitating
features of a spoken language (e.g., cadence, phrasing, and
intonation patterns).

HOW DOES MUSIC EXPRESS EMOTION?

Peter Mew offered an explanation that music may express
emotion without the "mediation of emotional objects"
(Mew, 1985, p. 33). He further wrote, "When a piece of

music arouses an emotion in a listener by or in directly expressing it the music acts as the *direct shaping voice* of the emotion: in a single movement the music both arouses and directly shapes the emotion" (Mew, 1985, p. 33).

Mew explained that music gives an expressive voice to the emotions. It awakens in the inner life emotion. But these are emotions initially without objects. Mew wrote, ". . . music arouses and gives expression to an objectless emotion before it induces [one] to think of any object(s)" (Mew, 1985, p. 34). Mew further recorded that "music presents feelings and invites objects," and in contrast, "literature and the visual arts present objects and invite feelings" (Mew, 1985, p. 34).

Roger Scruton (1983) sketched an objectivist position to musical expression. He believed that when we attribute sadness to a piece of music it is the result of our hearing sadness in the music. This attitude confines our interest to intrinsic qualities that are an end and not a means to evoking emotion. Osborne wrote that "the feelings we perceive in works of art are phenomenologically in the works and nowhere else" (Osborne, 1982, p. 20).

EXPRESSIONISM AND MUSICAL MEANING

Reimer (1970) contended that the absolute expressionist viewpoint about musical meaning is in accord with the absolute formalist in that meaning is to be found in the aesthetic qualities of the musical work. But the expression-ist extends those meanings to include a relation of art to life.

Reimer summarized this view: ". . . the aesthetic components in a work of art are similar in quality to the quality inherent in all human experience. When one shares the qualities contained in an art work's aesthetic content, one is also sharing in the qualities of which all human experience is made. The relation between the qualities of the art work and the qualities of human experience is felt by the perceiver of the work as 'significance' " (Reimer, 1970, pp. 24–25).

Another expressionist view concerning musical meaning

is that musical expression derives from the isomorphism between music and the emotions. Langer and followers, as modified expressionists, claim that music has meaning in that it reproduces the structure of the changing moods in life. The building up of tensions and the relaxation of tensions make for a kaleidoscope of temporal forms. It draws analogies between the musical structures and the contents of life's emotions (Osborne, 1982).

In *Philosophy on a New Key* Langer argues that music reflects the morphology of feeling. In *Feeling and Form* she demonstrates that music is the tonal analogue of emotive life. It is also believed that music shares some formal elements of the inner dynamics it symbolizes (e.g., patterns of motion and rest; tension and release; agreement and disagreement) (Hoaglund, 1980).

An alternative expressionist theory advocated by Kivy (1980) asserts that the music sounds like the gesture looks. Osborne wrote, ". . . the theory claims that our experience of feeling in music is to be accounted for by unconsciously perceived similarities between the 'shape' of the music and movements or postures of the human body which 'naturally' express emotion" (Osborne, 1982, p. 22).

This theory seeks resemblances between musical patterns and characteristic patterns of emotional expression in life. The music is expressive by congruence of musical "contour" with the structure of expressive features (Kivy, 1980). We hear the music as if it were a human gesture or utterance (Osborne, 1982). The composer creates musical gestures appropriate to the type of expression desired (e.g., sadness).

DERYCK COOKE AND REFERENTIALISM

Cooke (1959) stretched expressionism by developing a referential, hermeneutic theory of music that assigns specific emotional content to musical intervals. In *The Language of Music* (1959) Cooke offered an analysis of referential meaning in music. Cooke considered music to be a language that directly demonstrates actual feelings.

Specific intervals link up with specific emotional quali-ties. In an interpretation of this process Hoaglund re-corded, "The type of relation . . . that Deryck Cooke exhibits as holding between certain musical intervals and emotions are mere natural and mechanical sign associa-tions" (Hoaglund, 1980, p. 341).

Each musical interval represents a specific emotional state (e.g., the major third = a happy mood; the minor third = grief). Other elements of the music (e.g., tempo, dynamics, phrasing, and rhythm) give rise to qualities like tone-color and texture that illuminate the emotional effects (Sparshott, 1980). Bent described Cooke as one

> who argued for the materials of music as a quite specific vocabulary of intervallic contours with the connotations of emotional states. These connotations arise not by conven-tion but from the inherent forces of the intervals . . . . (Bent, 1987, p. 62)

THEORISTS WHO APPEAR TO BE CONGRUENT WITH MARXIST THEORIES

Marxist theories of music aesthetics, no matter how disparate, focus on the change music can accomplish in the recipient's consciousness. The Marxist contends that the musical art work, in effect, possesses an emancipatory impact on the recipient. Johnson wrote, "An account of the enlightening potential of the art work must attempt to find the foundations within the recipient's everyday conscious-ness for a new, emancipated way of thinking" (Johnson, 1984, p. 2).

In a statement of the process involved in ideological change Johnson further commented,

> A successful aesthetic theory needs to establish that the process of enlightenment does not merely involve the substitution of a correct consciousness, but crucially con-cerns the appropriateness of the response of the art work to the recipient's own dissatisfaction with his/her alienated consciousness. (Johnson, 1984, p. 2)

MARXIST PHILOSOPHY OF MUSIC AND REFERENTIALISM

The referentialist finds meaning outside of the musical art work. As referentialist one should go to the "ideas, emotions, attitudes, events, which the work refers you to in the world outside the art work" (Reimer, 1970, p. 15). The function of the art work is to inform one of the extramusical.

Reimer continued that for any referential theory, "the key factor of value is the non-aesthetic goodness of the art work's message." (Reimer, 1970, p. 15).

The Marxist finds meaning in the musical art work in that the work can potentially change the psyche of the listener. The Frankfurt School espoused that music can do this only when a progressive need for enlightenment has been established. They believed this has been essentially lost in modern, one-dimensional societies and it is their purpose to restore it (Johnson, 1984).

The humanistic position in Marxist aesthetics was advanced by Marcuse and Lukacs. Johnson wrote that "the ultimate goal of socialism must be conceived not only in economic and political terms but, centrally, as a matter of the emancipation of the alienated personality as well" (Johnson, 1984, p. 4). The work of Theodore Adorno best articulates the Frankfurt School's aesthetic position of humanism.

THEODORE ADORNO

Adorno's work has been called the most significant study of music and philosophy of the first half of the twentieth century (Culver, 1973). His work is the intellectual product of the Frankfurt School. With Horkheimer he constructed a critical theory that coupled the Marxist-Hegelian dialectical method with elements of Freudian psychoanalytical method.

The theory holds that laws, historical or natural, are beyond our conscious control. The loss of freedom in life causes an alienation of persons from their society. Such laws produce various historical tendencies in culture. Music reflects these tendencies and assumes similarities to cultural institutions from which they emanate (Culver, 1973).

Adorno's theory also encompasses the Hegelian principle that "contradiction is not external to reality but built into its structure" (Weitzman, 1971, p. 288). Adorno's work is marked by an existential involvement with the dialectic that holds music is simultaneously hermetically autonomous and socially interconnected (Blumenfeld, 1984). For Adorno, music, if it be true, must reflect society's dynamics as well as proceed from congeneric workings.

Weitzman judged that Adorno's work with the dialectics of music becomes clearer in the light of the psychoanalytical ideas of R. D. Laing. Laing advocated an existential phenomenology that attempts to characterize one's experience in the context of being-in-the-world (Weitzman, 1971).

Adorno and the culture industry. Adorno thought that mass culture causes a powerful manipulation of people's minds and creation of "false" needs for gratification (Johnson, 1984). The culture industry emerged in the twentieth century to predetermine the unconscious values of a usually unaware public. Adorno asserted that such manipulation of public taste causes regression in hearing and resistance to new or unfamiliar music. The public retreats to familiar musical patterns.

DaSilva also offered a description of Adorno's views of the culture industry:

> Horkheimer and Adorno speak of the ruthless unity in the culture industry wherein "something is provided for all so that none may escape." Just as propaganda artists pitch the same basic line to different audience, so the culture industry's stratagems bring the basic message—that the consumer must accept what industry provides—through various stylistic alternatives. (DaSilva et al., 1984, p. 83)

The culture industry creates the culture consumer. In his *Introduction to a Sociology of Music* (1976) Adorno outlined types of musical conduct. The types span a range from fully adequate listening to a total lack of understanding and complete indifference to the material. Type #3 in the book is the culture consumer. This is the type of listener who devours the dictates of culture.

Adorno wrote of this time, ". . . it substitutes hoarding as much musical information as possible, notably about biographical data and about the merits of interpreters, a subject for hours of inane discussion" (Adorno, 1976, pp. 6–7). The culture consumer places more satisfaction in the process of consumption than in the experiencing of the music. This type responds to the show ideal. The means to music (i.e., the technique) is an end in itself for the culture consumer. Conventionality and conformity are primary traits of their social character (Adorno, 1976).

It is expedient to cite Adorno's view of popular music within the context of the culture industry. He proposed that popular music was the result of an authoritarianism that is implicit in the culture industry. A constant, formularized message is presented to the public. Popular music never changes and its message of cultural conformity remains the same in spite of superficial variation (DaSilva, et al., 1984).

Adorno, historical musicology, and musical meaning. Like other Marxist aestheticians, Adorno challenged and was skeptical of historical musicology as a scientific discipline. Adorno endorsed the notion that history is art's most dangerous enemy. Sparshott wrote, "Marxist theory regards the postulated objectivity of musicological historiography as bourgeois mystification" (Sparshott, 1980, p. 129). Adorno opposed musicology's proclaiming certain interpretations of older music as definitive and authentic (Weitzman, 1971).

For Adorno, music of value resembles the dynamics of human progress, and the resistance to Western commercialism. Adorno in his Marxist position "abandoned historical materialism by assigning to the materia musica the resources available to the musical mind . . ." (Sparshott, 1980, p. 129).

Concerning musical meaning, Adorno believed that

meaning is contingent on the dialectic of the music. Meaning is not the result of pure presentations. A purist attitude towards music very often blocks the development of meaning in a work. Form manifests itself through the tension of a composition's essence and sensuous appearance (Adorno, 1967).

Adorno scrutinized the fallacy of the cultural critic. He wrote that critics speak as though their authority stems from objectivity and a higher sensibility. In fact, the critic is engaged in the same struggles as anyone else.

Adorno and tonality. Tonality in Western music is a by-product of a bourgeois era and the breakdown of tonality in the twentieth century is a sign of the breakdown of bourgeois society. Adorno believed the work of Schoenberg and Stravinsky reflects the sociological currents of our time (Adorno, 1973). Presenting the differences between Stravinsky and Schoenberg is the basis thesis of Adorno's *Philosophy of Modern Music.* Adorno advocated Schoenberg because he believed Schoenberg's work to be in harmony with the historical tendencies of his time (Adorno, 1973). The development of twelve-tone techniques represents a step for historical progress since Adorno thought dodecaphonic techniques were the logical consequence of tonality's disintegration.

Adorno (1973) held that Stravinsky's neoclassicism was fraudulent. Stravinsky, to the contrary, reflects the culture industry by acquiescing to its demands. Through a contrived musical style Stravinsky chose to defy history by ignoring the contradictions and antagonisms of contemporary society, and reverting back to an archaism that is embedded in concocted myth. Adorno pointed out that Stravinsky ignored the dialectic—the negativity in culture without which, Marxists believe, no culture can realize itself.

BALLANTINE AND THE DYNAMIC DIALECTICAL PROCESS

In *Music and Its Social Meanings*, Christopher Ballantine (1984) offered a rich semantic for musical reflection. He proposed that in order to more fully appreciate music's

significance one must penetrate the many levels of interpretation that are implied in the music. One such level is
the social meanings found in the music.

Unfortunately, the researcher is sometimes hindered in
this process because of preconceived views about music
that are considered universal and obvious. According to
Ballantine, these prejudices about music are more than
likely only reflective of our own age and will change with
the passage of time. Something which might be unthink-
able in one age is perfectly obvious and acceptable in
another time. He concluded that our unreflected-upon
attitudes about music are largely ideological (Ballantine,
1984).

The assumption that the nature of music is totally
detached from a life view is an example of an unquestioned
ideology that limits musicological inquiry. Musicologists
consider it obvious that musical research be disinterested,
abstract, and regarded for itself. He contradicted this view
by stating that music is a direct reflection of life and there
should be greater application of musico-philosophical
research (Ballantine, 1984).

Ballantine proposed to accomplish this by recovering
"the category of the dynamic totality; that is to say, to
group the concept of the whole (understood as being in a
process of change) and to situate it at the center of all our
discussions, all our thinking and doing in regard to our art
. . ." (Ballantine, 1984, p. 20).

The dynamic dialectical process based on a Marxist
model is central to Ballantine's thought. The researcher
who develops a sensitivity to the world-historical vision is
opening up to a richer semantic and ontology in the music.

PHENOMENOLOGY AND THE PHILOSOPHY OF MUSIC

WHAT IS PHENOMENOLOGY?

Phenomenology is a method by which one can study the
structure of knowledge. It is thought turned back upon
itself (DaSilva, et al., 1984). Its main interest is in elucidat-

ing assumptions. DaSilva wrote, ". . . phenomenology leads the individual thinker through mental experiments which set aside the contents or meanings of experiences and thoughts in order to look at the experiences and thoughts themselves" (DaSilva, et al., 1984, p. 21).

Ferrara noted,

> Phenomenologists presume that what one hears is affected by how one hears. The analyst's mode of orientation to a work must be considered and articulated. One can choose or open many potential meanings of a work given a particular mode of orientation. A distinctive phenomenological tactic is that, rather than manipulate a work through a formal grid of analytical questions or positions, one responds to questions posed by the work. The interpreter discovers that, in the traditional sense of the terms "subject" and "object," he is now object; the music, as "subject," questions the analyst. (Ferrara, 1984, p. 356)

Ferrara also wrote in *Qualitative Evaluation in the Arts,* (1981) "Phenomenological method is a mode of thought that opens one's consciousness to what is at hand to be experienced and provides a reflective process by which one can describe that previous, 'open' experience" (Ferrara, 1981, p. 130). The central feature of phenomenology is that reflective inquiry.

Phenomenology suggests a methodology that emphasizes the primordial immediacy of subjective experience. Through the phenomenological method one continually rediscovers and redefines the things experienced. The phenomenologist intuits essences (Jorgensen, 1976). Through the phenomenological method one suspends judgment concerning the relationships among variables.

There are several kinds of phenomenological approaches. Each of the leading theorists of phenomenology, which include Husserl, Heidegger, Merleau-Ponty, and Sartre, advocated a different brand of phenomenology. Nevertheless, each version considers the person and art works holistically. The phenomenologist assumes that persons and art works are greater than their parts. Ferrara's phenomenological approach has been cited as a most practical method for doing musical analysis (Cook, 1987). An overview of his method follows.

FERRARA'S MODEL FOR MUSICAL ANALYSIS

Ferrara's method for doing musical analysis can best be described as eclectic. He has set up an overall six-step process that includes a juxtaposition of traditional methods of musical analysis with phenomenological description. The analyst must be thoroughly grounded in the historical context in which the piece was composed. This includes an overview of the composer's corpus as well as a sense of the overall importance of the musical output.

Once accomplished, these data are put in abeyance as the analyst turns his/her attention to the work for its own sake. This is in keeping with the phenomenological operation of the epoche. This calls for a suspension of biases and prejudices whether positive or negative. Ferrara noted that such a suspension is relative; it is not possible to a tabula rasa stance toward anything. However, it is important to attempt to keep predisposition in check and to articulate its impact on the analysis.

The first step in the analysis is called open listening(s) (Ferrara, 1984). The purpose of these open listenings is to orient the listener and to allow any meanings in the work to unfold. Step two is in two parts. The first requires a traditional formal analysis of the piece. At this point the analyst can utilize any conventional system with which he is expert (i.e., Schenker, Meyer, Piston, LaRue, etc.). This is referred to by Ferrara as an analysis of the "sound in form." Remaining in step two, the analyst is asked to describe the "sound as such."

Ferrara noted that this is a more fundamental level of listening than hearing the sound in form. Ferrara noted, "To do so requires a bracketing out of one's formal training" (Ferrara, 1984, p. 359). To hear sound as such is not unlike the suggestion by Roman Ingarden that one should attend to a literary work, at a fundamental level of syntax, as a series of pure "word sounds." In hearing words as unalloyed phonemes, one attempts to bracket out the semantic (or referential) meanings that usually mark the process of listening to or reading ordinary language.

The unadulterated "word sounds" may give the literary critic a sense of the flowing quality or perhaps the jagged texture of a text that would not be as evident without such a hearing. In the case of a musical work, the results of such listening for a fundamental level of syntax can be an astounding experience of hearing sound purely as such. This kind of listening heretofore may have been more privy to very highly trained and sensitive musicians.

After all, great performers attend very carefully to the sound of their tone or to the texture of their sound (Ferrara, 1984). The language utilized for this second part of step two is usually highly metaphorical and therefore distinctive from the literal language utilized by traditional approaches to music analysis for a description of the "sound in form."

Step three requires a report of semantic meanings. Again this step is in two parts. The first part is a report of a program if one is present. In this case, as in program pieces like the *1812 Overture,* the representation may be more or less obvious. At the second stage of step three however, Ferrara asked the analyst to describe the feelings that are conveyed by the music. He took his use of the term "feelings" from Susanne Langer and so distinguished this usage as feelings that are virtual. Conveying Langer's insight, Ferrara noted that music transforms actual feelings into a symbolic or virtual form. These must be reported by the analyst.

Step four is a move into the ontological meaning of a work. Using Heidegger's philosophy as a metatheoretical structure Ferrara noted that great works of music "ground history." Ferrara explained, "As essential values, outlooks, decisions, potentials, and realities change, an ontological world of the composer's lived 'time' is to be grounded in those sounds." The musical work thus makes a 'new space' in sound for the composer's knowledge and experience of his or her world (Ferrara, 1984, p. 361).

Step five is a return to open listenings acknowledging the circularity inherent in any interpretive enterprise. By going from whole to part and back to whole the hermeneutic circle is accepted and allowed for by the method. Ferrara explained,

> The direction from the first "open" listenings to the final "open" listenings is thus circular. Each set of "open" listenings brackets the specific sets of syntactical, semantic and ontological listenings. The first "open" listenings are clearly peripheral to the potential meanings of the work. With each turn inward into the work—syntactical, semantic, and ontological—the analyst enters with increasing depth. Finally with the last "open" listenings (subsequent to the ontological listenings), the analysis is focused yet broad. The work stands as a living dynamic within the context of a clear and perhaps at times compelling gestalt. (Ferrara, 1984, p. 361)

Step six is entitled "metacritique." Here the analyst must discuss the inherent strengths and weaknesses of the analytical system and report the impact of those strengths and weaknesses on the analysis. Ferrara suggested that in evaluating an analysis the analyst must be able to move beyond the criterion of technical correctness. While it is important to check the data for its overall correctness Ferrara noted that what is most compelling in a great work is rarely simply correct or incorrect. He noted,

> The work and the analysis may both function at high levels of metaphor. Each is metaphorical in the sense that their respective meanings are not congenerically contained, but radiate outward to something other. The analysis and the work being studied are thus not two separate entities, closed in some definite space of finite meaning. Rather, each emits and resonates meanings that intersect in an ideational space. There is no quantitative correlation of correspondence truth between them; the "correctness" of the analysis cannot be measured against the work. (Ferrara, 1984, pp. 372–373)

Ferrara (1984) suggested that two criteria are possible: organicity and fecundity. To the degree that the analysis is grounded in the soil of the work, it is expressive of the work's message. Moreover, if the analysis is fruitful and spawns further insight and development of understanding toward this work, it is important.

The value of the phenomenological method is the openness it promotes. It is an openness that allows the syntax, semantic, and ontology to emerge. These elements are organically linked and grounded in the onto-historical world that yields a rich epistemological resource.

4. OVERVIEW OF LEADING PHILOSOPHIES OF MUSIC EDUCATION

The philosophies of music education very often probe the dynamic interrelationships of music and humanity. They recognize the problems concomitant to music education as aesthetic education and personal education (Schwadron, 1973).

Philosophical inquiry in music education promotes professional improvement and provides a rampart against the dynamics of accelerated change that exists in contemporary culture. The music educator hopefully comes to philosophy seeking critical bases for developing consistencies between the status quo and what is potentially possible (Schwadron, 1973).

THE THEORIES

POSITIVISM AND MUSIC EDUCATION

Ferrara (1982) instructed that positivism is a dominant philosophical ground for much experimental research in music education. Jorgensen (1976) concurred that positivism is one of the principal research orientations for music education.

Musical positivism generates objective, mathematical, analytical procedures as the source of value (McKay, 1958). The positivistic orientation stresses physiological and psychological information while virtually ignoring subjective data. It often makes the assumption that we can learn all there is to know about humanity by observing overt behavior. External behavior is considered the only indicator of a person's or situation's meaning.

The positivists fail to venture beyond appearances and do not penetrate, what they call, objective data in order to discover greater meaning in musical phenomena. This position is potentially weak in that it precludes subjective data, and thus, distorts reality.

The assumptions underlying positivism are incomplete since the positivist holds that discursive, logical reasoning is the only valuable form of intellection (Jorgensen, 1976). They ignore intuition and other forms of subjective knowledge, and consequently, rob the student of a potentially rich epistemological situation.

Concerning studies of the person, positivists think that a person can be studied atomically (i.e., the various parts of a person can be isolated and examined). Such piecemeal investigation is believed to yield the significant meaning of a person. This implies that a person or art work is equal to the sum of the parts examined; variables can reveal insight into totality. This implies that the methodology applicable to the study of physical phenomena is sufficient for the study of persons or art works (Jorgensen, 1976).

PHENOMENOLOGY AND MUSIC EDUCATION

Jorgensen wrote that phenomenological tradition is also an important theoretical methodology to educational research (Jorgensen, 1976). Phenomenological methodology is directly opposite from the positivistic stance. Unlike the positivists, the phenomenologist suspends conclusions concerning the relationship of variables. The phenomenologist comes to experiences free of all constraints, which are bracketed out.

Theorists, like Ferrara (1978), develop models for the practice of phenomenology in music education. The detailed explanation of Ferrara's approach, offered in chapter 3, is an example of a combination of eclectic modes and phenomenological method applied to music education.

AESTHETIC THEORIES

Schwadron (1967) grouped aesthetic theories into the following categories: complacency, eclecticism, isolationism, contextualism, and relativism.

COMPLACENCY

The complacent attitude espouses no philosophy of life or music. The complacent position precludes reliable standards of artistic value. It believes active commitment to a particular viewpoint is not feasible (Schwadron, 1967).

ECLECTICISM

Eclecticism acknowledges familiar philosophical views but like complacency excludes commitment to action. Ranking values is thwarted by the skeptic who offers no positive solutions to the many problems music education faces (Schwadron, 1967). The idea of synthesizing the best of several different styles or systems may seem appealing. However, while one may consider points from various philosophical schools, in the end people must make decisions that reveal a tendency to subscribe to a specific school of thought (Abeles et al., 1984).

ISOLATIONISM

The isolationist finds meaning in music only in congeneric terms. The isolationist is the purist, the absolutist, the formalist who believes music cannot have meaning in nonmusical terms. Musical meanings are found only in music materials and nothing more (Schwadron, 1967).

CONTEXTUALISM

For the contextualist, music is not an isolated phenomenon, but rather, it derives meanings from extramusical dimensions. The contextualist is concerned with how music interfaces with all forms of human behavior (e.g., education, psychology, morality, religion, economics, politics) (Schwadron, 1967).

RELATIVISM

For the relativist, musical meaning is dependent upon stylistic understanding and cultural orientation. Different critical positions are accepted on the basis of personal value systems. The relativist considers problems of musical value contingent on criteria drawn from personal evaluation. The relativist also purports that an individual's opinions need not possess universal or absolute validity (Schwadron, 1967).

Schwadron wrote, "He is not engaged in the philosophical pursuit of an absolute and universal value system, but in the logical recognition that values are relative to and conditioned by cultural groups and historical periods" (Schwadron, 1967, p. 44).

PHILOSOPHIES OF EDUCATION AND MUSIC EDUCATION

IDEALISM

"Truth" is the governing reality for the idealist. Since idealism contends that all reality is governed by a fixed spiritual dimension, one can find "truth" by focusing only outside human experience. Traditional cultural values, the importance of history, a moral sense derived from authority, as well as a feeling of predestination, are important components in the idealist's way of thinking (Samuelson, 1988).

Idealists concern themselves with questions of ethics and values (Abeles et al., 1984). Moral behavior is based on absolute regulatory rules. One is considered most moral when one conforms to the moral principles invested in and interpreted by authorities.

Value are immutable and become part of tradition. The ultimate purpose of education is to bring the uneducated (especially children) into conformity with ideal cultural values.

The teacher is the authoritative interpreter of all educational and societal expectations. There is little room for individualization. The student is expected to passively conform to educational standards set by the traditional teacher-authority. Ideal freedom is interpreted as conformity to the parameters set by higher authority or tradition. Consequently, the critic is viewed as a judge, a voice of authority who determines what is acceptable or unacceptable (Samuelson, 1988).

Knowledge is thought to be revealed to the student through vehicles of institution (e.g., histories, sacred works, authorities). Thus, the school curriculum is based on logical, cognitive, traditionally accepted practice and facts.

The idealist perceives physical objects as imperfect embodiments of the ideas they represent, which are universal and eternal (Abeles et al., 1984). Thus, truth is sought as the ultimate idea of a musical work.

Idealist music education focuses on the richness of masterpiece repertoire. Schwadron summarized the idealist's approach to music education. He wrote,

> The educational task of arousing emotional responses by means of exposure is then followed by systematic studies of the subtle characteristics and symbolic implications relevant to the music, the composer and the socio-cultural background. Foremost in promoting the development of such cultivated taste, the idealist holds to the mutual companionship of mind and feelings, for true taste and cultivated aesthetic enjoyment require exposure, objective mastery and finally understanding (Schwadron, 1967, p. 49).

REALISM

The realist perceives things as they appear to be, not representations of some greater invisible spiritual reality. Realists maintain that truth is discovered through scientific observation and method. They believe that truth can be found in nature and its laws.

Realists confirm the reality of the physical world beyond the mind, and the mirror-like character of the mind in receiving images which it then organizes and tries to interpret (Abeles et al., 1984). The world of real existence for the realist is independent of human intervention. Thus, value is thought to be found in the careful study of nature. Morality is believed to be contingent upon the discovery of natural laws. Traditions are developed in order to promote harmony between these natural laws and societal dynamics. Personal freedom within a social framework is only limited by nature since all creatures are subordinate to the laws of nature.

Epistemologically, the realist prioritizes knowledge that is based on the scientific, logical analysis of nature. Consequently, the school curriculum, which is usually very structured, emphasizes the development of skills necessary for the utilization of knowledge gained by scientific method. A critical attitude arises that often assesses natural dynamics and the arts' imitation of these relationships (Samuelson, 1988).

The realist's position in music education stresses the structural and formal principles of music. Applied music is favored since the sensuous, tactile approach to learning music is considered superior to passive listening. Broudy (1958) presented a realistic philosophy for music education by which connoisseurship is the standard in music. Connoisseurship implies growth in taste and appreciation as a correlative to growth in musical skill. It promotes the use of proven materials in music education. It evaluates them in terms of knowledge and cultivated taste (Leonhard, 1965).

Broudy (1958) also contended that in order for the teacher to be effective, the heritage of musical tradition within the framework of connoisseurship should be experienced by the teacher.

PRAGMATISM

Truth is a relative phenomenon for the pragmatist. It exists only as a by-product of the mind that employs experience, scientific method, and personal reflection in order to reconstruct reality (Samuelson, 1988). Ideas are valid only if they have practical value. Useful applications are favored over value judgments.

Morality is contingent on the interaction of the utilitarian needs of the individual and society. Ethical mores are not tied to absolute values. Values are derived from the interaction of the individual with the social environment (Samuelson, 1988).

Axiologically, values are relative. Pragmatism is a theory of human action that values cognitive knowledge. For the pragmatist, the process of thinking is more important than "static" knowledge.

McMurray (1958) outlined the principal conclusions of pragmatic inquiry: (1) To act deliberately with intent in mind; (2) To act knowing the consequences of our actions; (3) To consciously control one's feelings, actions, desires in order to achieve long-range goals.

Epistemologically, the pragmatist views knowledge as experience that is constantly changing. Phelps (1980) wrote that experience is thought to be either immediate (i.e., now) or mediated (i.e., the interaction of reflection and environment). Teachers are perceived as being more knowledgeable than students but share power and ideas with the student in a nonauthoritarian way (Samuelson, 1988).

Freedom is viewed as a quality by which one can create within a democratic sociopolitical context. The individual is encouraged to develop in order to contribute to society's improvement and overall good (Samuelson, 1988).

Because of its emphasis on practical considerations, pragmatism is a popular philosophical model for music educators. The music curriculum emphasizes performance skills and the gaining of information that promotes utilitarian ends.

McMurray wrote that the aim of music education is to (1) promote greater sensitivity to sound patterns as aesthetic phenomena; (2) help develop each person's potential to experience aesthetic richness through music; and finally, (3) helps shape public musical culture into a history of each person's environment (McMurray, 1958).

Both reconstructionism and utilitarianism are closely aligned with the pragmatic educational model.

Reconstructionism is essentially a kind of utopianism in that musical culture is examined in the light of its social responsibilities. Schwadron wrote,

> An aesthetic understanding of the world community would necessitate an intelligent socio-cultural and ethnomusicological study of economic, political, and religious aspects, value systems, class structures, family and leisure patterns, and historical traditions. (Schwadron, 1967)

For the reconstructionist, the purpose of music cannot be achieved unless the musician recognizes the necessity for social integration of music. The parameters of music education are broadened to include music's impact on all of society (Schwadron, 1967).

Fowler wrote, "Reconstructionism stands for a rethinking, a reshaping, and a repatterning of the existing order of world civilization. It asks that education assume responsibility for cultural development" (Fowler, 1988, p. 131).

Reconstructionism is an anthropologically centered philosophy in which the student is asked to engage in reshaping culture.

A utilitarian model for music education does not necessarily denote just the extrinsic benefits from music study but the "value of aesthetic development to the individual by extension to society" (Mark, 1988, p. 112). As the individual grows, so does the society benefit and improve. In this way, utilitarianism's paradigm can reconcile with aesthetic education models.

EXISTENTIALISM

The existentialist experiences truth as the product of individual inquiry. Truth is not absolute for it is based upon meanings that are personally relative (Samuelson, 1988). Since the individual is at the core of ontological meaning, the existentialist believes that one's being is the purpose of one's existence (Phelps, 1980). The self reveals the truth, and therefore, knowledge obtained through personal experience is valued above information revealed by sources outside of the self.

The highest moral good, for the existentialist, is the pursuit of fully developing the genuine self. "To be true to oneself" is a motivating maxim. Consequently, one focuses to achieve harmony within oneself (Samuelson, 1988).

Value evolves from individual decisions. The most valuable choices are those that help one to achieve authenticity. This is thought to enhance one's experience of freedom.

Ontologically, freedom, which is essential for the existentialist, means that one is totally free to meaningfully create oneself. It also implies that one must accept the consequences for one's decisions and actions. The existentialist's concept of freedom embraces intellectual, as well as physical, form. Thus, because the existentialist proposes that individuals should continually redefine themselves, change is an integral component for personal development (Samuelson, 1988).

An individual's meanings are more significant than meanings ascribed by outside forces. As a result, the critic's traditional role of communicating authoritative comment is considered unimportant and useless.

The purpose of education is to help the individual achieve self-sufficiency and authenticity. The existentialist teacher, in keeping with this concept, sees his or her role as a facilitator rather than an authority figure. The teacher ideally shares responsibility with the student as a coequal. Individual expression is encouraged and methods to stimulate independent thinking are employed. Axiologically, an arts-humanities curriculum is important because through these disciplines one's individuality can be most effectively voiced (Phelps, 1980).

One manifestation of existential thought in music education is the process of experimentation. The experimentalist rejects all absolutes. Values are considered subjective without reference to idealization. Aesthetic judgment is experiential. It is the by-product of the interaction of music and the person. The experimentalist hopes that this activity will yield new insights, meanings, and feelings, for the experimentalist believes that it is the task of music education to stimulate new meanings and feelings in the learner.

Under this rubric, the student is encouraged, like the realist, to study a musical instrument. The isolated music of the concert hall is thought to be nonconducive to the development of musical taste and knowledge. Direct contact with an instrument fosters understanding and acquired taste (Schwadron, 1967).

In addition to the theories cited above, Mark (1982) claimed that the prevailing philosophy of music education has evolved from a strong utilitarian base (as found in the literature of Madison, Mueller, McKay, Burmeister, House, and Gaston) to theories of aesthetic education as outlined in Reimer (1970).

Around the middle of the twentieth century there was a shift of focus in music education from attention to societal needs (e.g., music for ceremony, religion, patriotism) to aesthetic issues and goals. Aesthetics was considered the rationale for the justification of music education in formal institutions. Music, taught under this rubric, is for the sake of aesthetic development and not necessarily for the social importance of the aesthetically developed individual.

Reimer (1970) contributed to the literature of the philosophy of music education by offering an expressionist's philosophy of music education. There are four conceptual elements that earmark Reimer's theory: 1) mind as expressor; 2) learned object as expressed; 3) the art-work-product of expression; 4) the art-symbol. Reimer's theory features the art-symbol as the ontological basis for a philosophy of music education.

McKay (1958) mentioned *mysticism, vitalism, traditionalism, individualism,* and *humanism* as additional theories for the philosophy of music education.

The mystic believes that musical value comes from the unknown. Meaning is rooted in realities beyond the known world that cannot be discursively expressed. Logical procedure in art or education are ignored in the trust that truth will be experienced in the unknown.

Vitalism is a model by which the musician returns to the vigorous in primitive art. It uses a kind of pantheism as a source of value. The musician, under this modus, probes more vital life expressions in art. Delius, Debussy, and other impressionists sought this kind of value in their art work. Vitalism can also be observed in the modern trends towards presenting primitive style music (e.g., Orff, minimalists).

The traditionalist turns to the past for inspiration. Stravinsky (1947) declared that tradition is the only genuine means to artistic freedom. He explained that tradition is that volume of practice which is integral to art in spite of the philosophical flux in contemporary music.

Value, for the traditionalist, comes from the wisdom of past ages that gathers into a solid, reliable knowledge. Composers who work under the neoclassical model (e.g., Hindemith, Harris, Schuman, Piston, Carter, and Britten) are traditionalists in countenance. Oftentimes, traditionalism is associated with the attitude that professes that great art is somehow the product of aristocratic intelligence.

Individualism is in direct contrast to traditionalism. The basic premise of individualism is invention, which involves individuality and innovation. Charles Ives is an example of a composer who was dedicated to rugged individualism.

Humanism seeks out the common person as a source of the highest value, and thus, is opposed to the traditionalist's notion that great art can only emanate from the aristocratic intelligence. The humanist sees value as naked humanity in all of its assets and liabilities, its heroic and baser moments.

A DEVELOPMENTAL PHILOSOPHY OF MUSIC EDUCATION

James L. Mursell (1934, 1958) offered a developmental philosophy of music education. He was basically influenced by the work of Montessori and Piaget in educational psychology. Mursell, as humanist, brought the benefits of Gestalt psychology to music education. He proposed that all significant educational values evolve from human values. His foremost assumption for the philosophy of

music education is that the individual should possess a
primary value system. Music's intrinsic value is as a means
for fostering growth in human potential.

The notions cited above emanate from developmental
psychology and progressive education's concept that education is ideally a form of guidance for personal growth.
Through effective music education one's personality ideally moves towards new orientations that predispose one to
experience fulfillment (Mursell, 1948).

Five principles emerge from Mursell's philosophy of
music education: (1) one should possess a philosophical
orientation to the teaching of music; (2) experiences that
promote achievement in personal living should be provided; (3) self-discipline should be advocated; (4) social
development should be promoted by means of advocating
social relationships and experiences; and (5) education
should widen cultural horizons.

What types of musical activity did Mursell advocate in an
educational setting? Mursell felt that listening should
penetrate all musical activity. The type of listening he
advocated was a developmental type of inner listening in
which the sound is imagined apart from its physical
manifestation. Because the voice possesses human quality,
Mursell advocated that singing should be the main activity
in music education.

Integration in education should occur within people, not
subject matter (Mursell, 1965). Mursell presumed, as did
Plato, that music promotes personal growth because it
instructs one's emotional life. Music, of all the arts, has
most relevance to human values because the phenomenon
of tone is the most connected with the emotions (Mursell,
1934).

Schwadron (1967) made the following observations in
demonstrating a parallel between aesthetic and educational theories. The theory of relativism corresponds to
reconstructionism in that both turn from absolute theories
of value and acknowledge that educational process is
contingent upon historical and cultural factors.

While isolationism and contextualism seek absolute
value, relativism is drawn to criteria that are relative to a

specific historical and cultural context. In conclusion, Schwadron (1967) pointed out that aesthetic problems cannot be separated from other questions in music education. Aesthetic inquiry's mission is to uncover new modalities through multidimensional discussion.

5. THEMES FROM GOULD'S WRITINGS TOWARD A PHILOSOPHY OF MUSIC AND MUSIC EDUCATION

The themes about music found in Gould's writings encompass a wide range of thought. He did not limit his commentary to discussions about music's intrinsic dynamics. Rather, he expanded his musical vision to include discourse with ethical, social, and educational ideas. Within the context of this approach, music is juxtaposed with other intellectual dimensions and developed in various thought contexts. Music does not exist in an isolated vacuum but is a phenomenon of dynamic process that involves many spheres of thought (De Jager, 1974). Gould understood this, and thus, wrote from an aesthetic position that expansively dealt with and penetrated music as well as other facets of knowledge.

The themes found in Gould's writings are organized into the following categories: (1) Ideas for a Social Philosophy of Music; (2) Ideas for a Theory of Music; (3) Ideas for a Theory of Music Criticism; (4) Ideas for an Epistemology of Music; and (5) Ideas for a Morality of Music.

IDEAS FOR A SOCIAL PHILOSOPHY OF MUSIC

Gould assigned great importance to the relationship of art to society because he concluded that art was a powerful social force. Gould believed art influences people's lives and reaches their spiritual roots and concomitant social manifestations. Consequently, Gould (1976a) proposed that the artist should be granted a recognized and respected role by society.

Gould was critical of cultures that stripped the artist of qualities important to the fully functioning artistic temperament and role. He believed that the Soviet Union was a good example of a culture that distorts and narrowly limits the artistic potential in practitioners of art. He wrote,

> . . . above all, it [U.S.S.R.] makes superficial and self-conscious all that is most genuine in the character of the artist—the unconscious, indeterminate subliminal relationship of a man's work to the society from which he comes. (Gould, 1984b, p. 171)

Gould believed that art was a direct and accurate reflection of the social dynamics of society. He saw an intimate connection between logical growth factors in art and our understanding of the history of society. Gould thought this is illustrated most clearly when artistic values of societies we consider to be civilized are compared to societies we regard as primitive (Gould, undated, Anthology of variation).

Status Hierarchy

Within the sociomusical model there exists a status-hierarchy (De Jager, 1974). Gould did not accept at face value the traditional status-hierarchy often implicit in the culturally conditioned world of classical music. He found such a hierarchy contrived and very often self-defeating. Gould described this structure of musical society under conventional circumstances as follows.

The center of the conventional musical society is the public concert hall. It is there that the sociomusical hierarchy focuses its energies. This status-hierarchical structure can be broken down into the following groups: composers, performers, listeners, and managers and public relations (the most powerful and the least articulately musical of the four groups) (Gould, 1964a). In this unnatural hierarchy, the participants assume predictable,

well-defined but separate status roles. Gould would probably concur that the unique role ascribed to each participant
in this structure is aptly described when Helm said, "The
composer creates, the performer re-creates, and the public
receives" (Helm, 1970, p. 9). Each participant's role has an
implicit status connected to it that defines the duties and
privileges as well as the limitations of the participants.

These traditional roles and their parameters set by
society are often considered safe haven by musicians. The
possible abolition of these roles is perceived by some as a
threat to the musical world. But, on closer deliberation of
the history of music, one discovers that institutions such as
the concert hall, with all of its attendant participants, are
fabrications of the nineteenth century. The actual institution of music making predates these sociomusical practices.
Because of its very nature, music can supercede and
survive institutions framed during certain time periods
(Ford, 1982).

In the traditional status-hierarchy model, participants'
roles are oftentimes the expression of a high degree of
specialization. This post-Renaissance specialization is so
great that it can actually interfere with the smooth
operation of a well-functioning musical society. The integrated communication necessary in a dynamic musical
society often breaks down because of this specialization. It
often isolates the specialist who can only perform under
rigid, separate professional parameters. The necessary
integration of participants is blocked by this specialization
and, sometimes, causes the groups to work against each
other and become counterproductive to the intended
artistic goals (e.g., the composer Milton Babbitt uses
methods that appear to be much more interested in the
musical art work than in the problems of communicating
that art work to the listener) (Griffiths, 1981). Apparently,
he has isolated the composer's role from the listener to the
extent that the listener is virtually excluded from the
sociomusical chain and that chain is weakened.

Gould objected to the self-limiting roles of an overspe-
cialized musical society and its iron-clad traditions. He

believed that participants in the musical society can cross
the barriers of specialization with success. As an example
he described the creative situation of Walter Carlos's
production of the *Switched-On Bach* album. He thought
that, in spite of the lack of specialization of roles, it was
possible for Walter Carlos to produce a highly successful
recording that was an example and potential prototype for
future endeavors. Gould stated,

> . . . the "performer" for *Switched-On Bach* . . . is no
> professional virtuoso taking time out from the winter tour
> for a visit to the recording studio but a young American
> physicist and audio engineer named Walter Carlos, who
> has no recording contract, whose most esoteric musical
> endeavor heretofore was the supervision of sound track
> material for a Schaeffer beer commercial on T.V. (Gould,
> 1968, p. 54)

Gould (1984b, 1965a) was not happy with the tensions
created by specialization and other factors in the traditional status-hierarchy of the music world. He thought that
the artist should have the freedom to work in anonymity
unaware of the stressful demands of the marketplace. He
also believed that such counterproductive pressures could
disappear if a sufficient number of artists would abandon
their false sense of public responsibility. Conversely, if the
artist would follow personal inspiration instead of public
demands the public could consequently relinquish its role
of servile dependency. Nevertheless, he also realized that
the status-hierarchy of the music world is not easily broken
down since it promotes its own arcane cult, credos,
mysteries, and methods that are guarded and preserved.

By questioning the qualities inherent in the stratified
professionalism of occidental music, Gould promoted
knowledge towards the necessary functional integration
among participants. He offered ideas for changing the
status-hierarchy of the music world and challenged the
traditional values therein that perpetuated this system. But
he also implied that it was not clear in his own mind
whether he was totally justified in doing this. He wrote,

> You're not quite sure whether in making that mystery explicit, in exploiting the dichotomy between layman and professional, we do our fellow man a service or a disservice. You're not quite sure whether in opting for an environmental course, which, after all puts an end to professionalism as we know it, we're getting at some truth about ourselves more immediate than any professional can achieve, or whether, in doing that, we're simply reining in our own development as human beings. (Gould, 1972, p. 5)

Gould was not alone in sounding death knells for the traditional sociomusical groups. Other Canadian musicians of note have expressed similar viewpoints (e.g., R. Murray Schafer commented that the composer's traditional role will no longer be needed in the future since the availability of mass repertoire through recording has changed musical society) (Ford, 1982). On a similar note, Arnold Walter (1957) said that if all of the world's composers dropped dead, the ordinary listener would not notice it for years.

Gould was also reflecting, like so many contemporary composers, the "music as environment" views of American avant-garde composer and theorist John Cage. Cage, through the composition of pieces like *4'33"*, made an important contribution to the philosophy of music by radically redefining what music was, and thus, he irrevocably changed music's direction in contemporary culture.

Cage's ideas changed the dialectical character of music in that the struggle of form and content disappears. With this, the historicity of a work fades in favor of the absolute reality of the music's immediate experience (Mertens, 1983).

Inspired by such contemporary aesthetics, Gould developed ideas that attempted to reshape the status-hierarchical parameters for participants in the music world. For the most part, these ideas stem from Gould's practical knowledge and intuition as an artist. The following is a detailed examination of ideas concerning the hierarchical sociomusical structure. Gould restricted his discussions to include commentary about the performer, listener, composer, and musical institutions.

THE COMPOSER

Gould (1964i) maintained that the relationship of the composer to a society cannot be determined by the assumption that the composer is best who conforms to the interests of that society. It is indeed possible for composers to step out of their chronological times and generate work that will have more effect on many generations after their own time, as in the case of J. S. Bach. Gould asserted that this phenomenon challenges the opinion that the art of the present is necessary for the artistic health of the community.

Gould (1972) believed that composers should possess the following qualities in their work. It should be economical, unheroic, balanced, and tonally ambivalent on occasion, when tonality is involved. In addition, Gould (1953b) thought the ideal composer should crystallize physical and spiritual experiences through artistic expression. One can observe from this list and his other writings that Gould favored qualities in composition that undermined the theatrical or showy and emphasized the spiritual, introspective, and transcendent.

He also concluded that the composers who transcended the musical styles and dogmatic adherences of their age made richer their own time by being removed from it. The composer who speaks to all ages by being all ages is eternally individual and relevant (Gould, 1961).

Gould (1983a) proposed that the composer's role is contingent upon our concept of music. If music's parameters include only sounds that are selected and absolutely controlled by the composer's will, then the composer has ultimate power over the decisions of the performer, who more than likely acquiesces to the composer's literal dictates. Gould compared this process with the operations of the nineteenth-century general who commanded and held everything together.

Gould cited the composer of the sonata-allegro form as a good example of the composer who dominates all facets of the artistic process. Gould said in an interview with Curtis Davis that, within this context, the composer has such supreme power over the material "he could . . . by textural alterations, by changes of pace, by all of the things of which a sonata or a symphony could be disrupted, and the events, the whole course of events changed . . . he could . . . demythologize his characters" (Gould & Davis, 1983a, p. 289). Gould further commented that "he [the composer] could actually make one feel a sense of metamorphosis, a sense of implicit plot context in relation to what he was doing" (Gould & Davis, 1983a, p. 289). This type of composer could be characterized as aggressive in the manipulation of the composition's materials.

But, if one's concept of music is different and music includes all the available sounds of the environment then the composer exercises only limited control over the materials of the composition since one cannot absolutely control the randomness of environmental events. Within this model for creativity, the environmental ecology is as influential in the artistic product as the composer. Gould demonstrated he was inclined to support this vision of music by the following quote: "I think our whole notion of what music is has forever merged with all the sounds that are around us—everything that the environment makes available. . ." (Gould & Davis, 1983a, p. 280).

In the above quote, this author believes to have an important key to understanding Gould's convictions about composition as well as performance. He claimed that creativity did not necessarily have to be, indeed, could not be the product of a sole, god-like creator. Rather, creativity involved the influences of multiple environmental factors. In addition, if one accepts the extended parameters of music to include more than a manifestation of an individual composer's psyche and will, then acceptance of shared artistic decisions with others is not only possible but desirable.

Gould argued it was opportune for a composer to share creative responsibility for a number of reasons. First, he believed that the anonymity achieved by multiple authorship would shift interest from biographical data to the work itself. Since chronological detail depends upon knowing who the creator is and when in time the work was created, not knowing these facts would eliminate distracting biographical detail and free the observer to focus on the art work. In describing this process he wrote,

> . . . the more participants you permit into the creative act, the more anonymity is automatically ceded to the individual participant—the more unlikely it becomes that we will find the need for those specific forms of information and biography which tended to determine to such a large extent our rather snobbish notions of historical progressivism. (Gould, 1964a, p. 27)

Gould was clearly opposed to a biography-obsessed musical society. He perceived that this was a superficial approach to music and objected to a culture whose judgment of art works was based on historical and chronological information rather than observation of the work itself.

Another outgrowth of the nonchronological orientation proposed by Gould (1975d) manifested itself in Gould's predilection for less popular, and often controversial, composers like Paul Hindemith, Ernst Krenek, Jean Sibelius, and Richard Strauss. Gould favored these composers because they seemed to go against the grain of historical progressivism. He considered them as an important "backwater" for the compositional climate of their times. They seemingly helped to put other composers in artistic relief. And, finally, they were often the antithesis of the artist as egoist. They epitomized a nonnarcissistic quality Gould considered very important in the sociomusical status-hierarchy paradigm.

The second reason Gould offered to justify shared authorship had to do with the composer and aggressive behavior. Gould claimed that aggression does not have a place in art because it is morally incompatible with his vision of art as transcendent activity. In relinquishing the exclusive rights of creative judgment the composer also sheds the tendency to exercise aggressive behavior since group decisions involve compromising the wills of more than one person.

The composer, in Gould's (& Davis, 1983a) sociomusical hierarchy, no longer assumes a god-like superiority by aggressively being the sole manipulator of the materials of composition. The composer no longer exercises an unalterable and absolute will (Gould, 1956f, liner notes from Columbia ML 5060). Rather, the composer shares and overlaps operations with the performer, the listener, and others involved in the creative process. This is especially true when the composer works in the electronic medium.

Gould thought that the electronic transmission of sound inspired multiple authorship in music. As a consequence, the electronic age has changed values about music. In addition, Gould proposed that one could no longer examine electronic culture in terms of invention, originality, or imitation. These concepts when used with the electronic culture are no longer capable of conveying the precise analytical meanings they once possessed (Gould, 1964f). He said further, "implicit in electronic culture is an acceptance of the idea of multilevel participation in the creative process" (Gould, 1964f, p. 59).

The third reason why Gould favored multiple authorship was the fact that individual opinion is redefined. "The whole process of individuality in the creative situation—the process through which the creative act results from, absorbs, and re-forms individual opinion—is subject to radical reconsideration" (Gould, 1966c, p. 63). Gould found it artistically liberating for the ego to be absorbed in a kind of medieval group consciousness. The individual could create in a milieu of relative anonymity and peace.

The fourth reason why Gould (1964i) maintained that multiple authorship was superior was that it weakens the artificially implied superiority of participants in the sociomusical hierarchy. Authority is shared by all and egocentric behavior is undermined.

Gould cited privacy as another by-product of the composer's acquiescence of absolute power over the musical art work. It is the final reason why Gould considered multiple authorship desirable. He wrote that the paradoxical creation of privacy was the most important contribution of the electronic culture to the arts. As a consequence, standards of artistic judgment have changed and artistic responsibility has shifted (Gould, 1964f).

This privacy extends from the composer to the audience. Gould continued,

> The great paradox about the electronic transmission of musical sound is that as it makes available to the most enormous audience, either simultaneously or in a delayed encounter, the identical musical experience, it encourages that audience to react not as captives and automatons but as individuals capable of an unprecedented spontaneity of judgment. This is because the most public transmission can be encountered in the most private circumstances. . . . (Gould, 1964f, p. 59)

Finally, Gould believed that inside each composer was a kind of inventor in competition with a museum curator. Within the compositional process a dialectic of opposing forces and roles was in constant flux. He imagined that most of the great events in music are the by-product of a temporary gain by one attitude at the expense of the other (Gould, undated, "Glenn Gould on Closed-Circuit T.V.— Part Three").

THE PERFORMING ARTIST

In order for a performer to be an artist the performer must be in a state of continuous spiritual change. One cannot be fixed or rigid in artistic concept, but one must be open and pliable. Every artist must be in a state of flux; otherwise, the artist compromises the true character of the creative experience (Gould, 1972).

In spite of the above statement, Gould (1978g) maintained that it is possible to divide and group performers into two categories. First are those musicians who seek to exploit the musical instrument that they use. These are musicians who allow their relationship with the instrument to become the focus of their attention. In addition, they are determined to make us aware of this relationship to their instrument. Second are those musicians who do not exploit the instrument that they use. Gould said that these musicians try to bypass their instruments and create an illusion that there is a direct link between themselves and the score. They perform in order to involve the listener with the music rather than the performance of the music for its own sake. Gould cited Sviatoslav Richter as a typical example of this second type of performing musician.

Gould wrote that Richter achieved such a perfect connection with the piano that the mechanical and physical processes involved were totally subordinated to the musical structure. As a result, the performer and listener were able to virtually ignore Richter's virtuosic features and were able to concentrate on the spiritual qualities inherent in the music.

Gould (1978g) considered Richter's approach towards music to be an ideal one. Richter's modus operandi inserts between the composer and listener a strong personality that serves as a kind of conduit for new perspectives of a musical work. Indeed, Gould (1956) theorized that one's whole personality is tied up in performance.

Important qualities for the performer. When asked what were the most important facets of a musical personality Gould (1956b) responded that extreme concentration, perfect pitch, and an excellent musical memory were indispensable qualities. The following commentary demonstrates that Gould also valued other qualities and characteristics in the performing artist.

Gould (1974b) was opposed to any kind of ego gratification on the part of the performing artist. He held that the performing artist should focus attention on the musical composition and not on personal display.

Gould elevated the role of the performer to someone who should be more concerned with the development of musical and spiritual ideas rather than the physical manifestations connected with music making. He put this idea into practice especially in his mature years. It was then that he would learn a score by first committing it to memory and later playing it on the piano (Cott, 1984). He described his method as follows: ". . . about two or three weeks before I was to play the thing for the first time, I started to study the score, and about a week ahead of time I started to practice it (which sounds suicidal, but that's the way I always operate)" (Cott, 1984, p. 38).

Gould (1978e) contended that the musical performer should possess an ecstatic attitude when performing. This quality of ecstasy should also be a dimension of the performance phenomenon. According to Gould (1973d), the performer who is in a state of ecstasy functions on a level of transcendence, the highest level of consciousness. But before one can experience artistic ecstasy one must experience solitude.

In solitude, a prerequisite for ecstasy, one can experience an ecstatic state that frees one from self. In this ideal disposition, the performer goes beyond a mere mechanical reproduction of the musical notation (Gould, 1977c). This is another indication that Gould emphasized the spiritual rather than the material in art. He, thus, favored a nonmechanical approach rather than a mechanical conception of life.

Gould cited faith as another desirable quality for the performer. The performer should possess a faith that believes that what is being done is the right thing. The performer should approach the performance project with a great sense of personal individuality, purpose, and conviction. The performer should possess a faith in the potentiality of finding interpretive possibilities not wholly realized even by the composer (Gould, undated, media transcript, "Glenn Gould interviewed by Bernard Asbell"). This faith holds that the physical fact of music making is unimportant since through faith one can leap into more important dimensions. Gould (1976f) cited artists like Menuhin, Schweitzer, and Casals as examples of artists who possessed an artistic faith that was spiritually transcendent.

In such a state of spiritual transcendence the artist-performer might achieve a spiritual transfiguration larger than life. Such a view of art made it an instrument of salvation and the artist the missionary advocate (Gould, 1966f). The artist should also be prepared to sacrifice personal comfort to achieve these ideals of musical and spiritual integrity (Gould, 1984b). Since the most genuine characteristic of the artist is the unconscious, indeterminate, subliminal relationship of the artist's work to the society from which the artist comes, Gould (1984b) considered it important.

Finally, Gould thought that imagery should be at the core of the artist's performance practice. He utilized this approach and believed it to be ideal (Cott, 1984). He explained that it was more imagery than tactile practice that was the basis for his performance practice (Dubal, 1984). He believed in divorcing tactilia from expressive manifestations of one kind of another. In explanation he said, ". . . certain expressive manifestations were built into the analytical concept, but the tactile assumptions were not" (Cott, 1984, pp. 37–38).

When one exercises imagery in performance one should not move the fingers. Gould was certain that if you move your fingers you will automatically reflect the most recent tactile impressions that you have been exposed to (Cott, 1984). The more ideal situation would be to have a sufficient concept in advance or an extratactile experience of the music so that "anything the piano does isn't permitted to get in the way" (Cott, 1984, p. 40). If the instrument is a difficult one to manage the imagery, the memory of a more compliant action will rescue the performer from an almost impossible performance situation.

Gould also proposed that analytical completeness could be achieved as long as one studied the score away from the instrument. As soon as tactile factors were involved the concept of the musical structure would be compromised and diminished. This was considered important since Gould believed that one changes one's approach to the music's structure according to the analytical method one employs (Cott, 1984).

Audience and performer. Gould (1974b) was not content with the implications concerning an audience and the performing artist. He held that performing before a live audience had too many drawbacks that distracted the artist from total involvement in the artistic image. He stated that the artist should be able to work in the freedom of anonymity. Gould (1981) proposed that because of such anonymity the performer does not have to worry about trivia like nerves or finger slips. The performer would not have to anxiously be concerned with the naked fact of humanity on display unedited and unadorned. Gould (1980d) attested that he never felt better about the quality of a performance because of the presence of an audience.

Gould was not comfortable with the limited boundaries imposed on the artist performing in live settings. He found that giving live concerts was a distasteful and degrading experience. He said that concerts were a poor substitute for real artistic experiences (Gould, 1980d, media transcript, "Glenn Gould interviewed by Elye Mach"). Gould believed that the artist is more concerned with audience reaction at live concerts than artistic expression. He cited his experiences with performing Bach's *Fifth Partita* as a typical example. He wrote, ". . . the Fifth Partita was a real party piece in those days and the recording showed all the disadvantages of concert experience—all the seamy little tricks of projection that one thinks one needs—and, indeed one does need—to reach the top balcony in a concert hall" (Gould, undated, media script, "Gould interviewed by Andrew Marshall," p. 21).

The performing artist and isolation. Gould imagined that the performing artist works better in isolation. Gould wrote that in such an environment the knowledge of the outside world is always filtered by editorial control and "never permitted to intrude upon the indivisibility of that unit formed by the artist's idea and its execution" (Gould, 1977c, p. 7). Certain kinds of isolation tend to stimulate the creative mentality and are valuable to the performer for that reason. Isolation also generates an idealistic alternative within the artistic atmosphere (Gould, 1984b). Finally, Gould claimed that the isolation of anonymity negates and transcends the competitive intimidation of chronology (Gould, 1973c).

Gould thought that in order for a performing artist to produce worthwhile work it is necessary for the artist to be a bit of a bad social being. He wrote, when in his twenties,

"I've taken long walks by myself ever since I can remember. I'm not anti-social, but if an artist wants to use his mind for creative work then self-discipline, in the form of cutting oneself off from society, is a necessary thing" (Gould, 1956d, p. 7).

The performing artist and recording. The recording studio seemed to be the ideal setting for performing artist to achieve artistic goals without the distractions and stresses of live audience contact.

Within the isolation of the recording studio, Gould (1966d) said that the performer could be independent of interpretive gestures that might detract from the artistic intention. These gestures are inevitably developed in order to win over the upper balcony. They include very often pieces that are overplayed because the artist knows that they are a sure thing for success with the audience. In addition, characteristics in playing are oftentimes intuitive compensations for an acoustic dilemma. The performer creates certain musical distortions in the musical structure in order to overcome acoustic problems like poor instruments, or poor placement of instruments.

Gould (1966d) pointed out that the recording artist also developed some interpretive gestures that respond not to the audience but to the microphone's special demands. As an example of this phenomenon Gould cited Robert Craft's recordings. Gould ascertained that these recordings tell us much about the way in which performances prepared with the microphone can be influenced by technological considerations.

Two additional advantages for the performer as recording artist are the capability of post-facto judgment, and the ability to dissect music in strong, analytical, conceptual terms. The recording artist can engage in post-facto judgment as opposed to the frantic decision making of the live concert stage. Thus, the performer can remain more readily faithful to the artistic vision because of the capability of post-facto judgment (Gould, 1983a).

Through technological intervention the performer is capable of dissecting the music and presenting it in strongly biased, conceptual terms that the private and concentrated circumstances of the listener make feasible. Gould claimed,

> whether one arrives at such a conviction pretaping or posttaping (another of the time-transcending luxuries of recording: the posttaping reconsideration of performance), its existence is what matters, not the means by which it is effected. (Gould, 1966d, p. 52)

Gould (1966d) declared that recording has altered our notions about what is appropriate to the performance of music. Gould offered the following reasons how this is so: (1) Stratagems that are appropriate to fulfill the acoustical and psychological requirements of the live concert are not appropriate when subjected to the repeated playbacks of recording. They are irritating and antiarchitectural.

When the performer thinks in terms of recording, (2) the performer is challenged by the stimulus of unexplored repertoire; (3) the performer is expected to undertake the recording of the complete works of a composer; (4) the functions of the performer overlap with the tape editor. Gould said, ". . . when the performer makes use of the post performance editorial decisions, his role is no longer compartmentalized" (Gould, 1966d, p. 53). The music is no longer presented through the exclusive mediation of the performer but is shared with an invisible network of recording professionals that make artistic decisions in relative anonymity (Gould, 1982c).

(5) The authority of the performer yields to the producer and tape editor (Gould, 1966d). And finally, Gould said that, (6) the performer-listener relationship through recording enables both the performer and the listener to achieve a unique closeness. They are detached yet immediate and close because of the medium (Gould, 1980e).

The performing artist and puritan social values. Gould (1983a) was intrigued by and identified with puritan social values. Indeed, he called himself the "last puritan." In describing the puritan viewpoint of the artist-performer, Gould said that the artist was either thought of as a channel for damnation or viewed as a kind of redeemer. It was a common idea that the artist put one needlessly in the way of damnation. This meant that the artist was catalyst to exposing one to the temptations of sinister thoughts. Because the artist must live with these troubling thoughts, in the end, seduction would be inevitable (Gould, 1966f). Gould viewed this image of the artist as a jeopardized being to be strikingly viable and psychologically accurate.

Gould (1984b) held to the viewpoint that the artist wielded demonic power. This view implicitly conveys a respect for the artist's social role. It bestows upon the performer-artist a role that is far beyond the contemporary egalitarian affection. But, on the other hand, Gould contended that puritan societies could breed rare artists that would also be cultural redeemers. He wrote,

> in puritan societies a rather unique bargain was sometimes struck and this allowed that, given exceptional circumstances, the society could breed a very rare type of artist, an artist capable of witnessing to some sort of spiritual transfiguration for which his art could be conduit. And this, of course, was the view of art as an instrument of salvation and the artist as missionary-advocate. (Gould, 1976a, p. 5).

Spiritual transcendence was important for Gould. He wrote that the uncommon artist is potentially able to achieve a kind of spiritual transfiguration that is the direct product of artistic transcendence (Gould, 1966f).

In the puritan society censorship conveys a respect for the performing artist's role that is often lacking in other cultures.

> Just as censorship, that ultimate weapon in the puritan missile system, flatters the power of words to infect and inflame in a way that the laissez-faire of the liberal literati never can, this view of the artist as wielder of demonic power, as a being whom ordinary mortals should approach with caution, implicitly conveys a respect for his role beyond that egalitarian affection with which today's unionized troubadour is casually welcomed with the fold of the community. (Gould, 1966f, p. 8)

Puritan societies were pragmatic entities that constantly needed to redefine their highest purposes (Gould, 1966f).

Gould believed (1984b, 1966a, 1974b, 1964a) that audiences were growing bored with the conventions of the musical establishment. Consequently, a new kind of listener was emerging. The new listener would assume a more active role in the hierarchy of the sociomusical society. This was especially true with the intervention of the electronic medium. Because of the electronic medium the listener could assume a more active role in music. The listener could cease being an automaton in relation to the music.

The listener could be a creative listener whose reactions to the music could be earmarked by unique insights not originated in the performer or other music makers. These insights initiate a new link in the sociomusical network. The listener would be well informed and capable of an analytical point of view (Gould, 1982c, 1983a).

The creative listener would be able to bracket out sounds in order to understand them in a phenomenological way (Gould, 1983a; Ferrara, 1982). The new, informed listener is also capable of focusing on syntactic structures dipping in and out of the musical experience (Gould, 1983a).

At home the listener could experience technical, however limited, and critical judgment via the controls of the playback equipment (Gould, 1964f). The electronic equipment encourages the listener/audience to shed its role of captive automaton and exercise unprecedented spontaneity of judgment (Gould, 1964f). Gould (1964a) claimed that the listener could experience music in a private setting and respond to the music in a personal way that could never be achieved with the mass response of the public audience. It was this change in audience's behavior that was the most fundamental change occasioned by the electronic presentation of music.

Gould went a step further and suggested that public

audience response should be eliminated entirely. He wrote,

> I am disposed toward this view because I believe that the justification of art is the internal combustion it ignites in the hearts of men and not its shallow, externalized public manifestations. The purpose of art is not the release of a momentary ejection of adrenaline but is, rather, the gradual, life-long construction of a state of wonder and serenity. (Gould, 1984b, p. 246)

Gould declared that the theatrical elements of the live concert presentation, including applause, corrupt the musical and spiritual side of the artistic experience.

Gould (1965c) also questioned how participant the listener could be as a member of a public audience. Gould emphasized that the public audience was limiting. It was not only unnecessary but bothering since it contributes to diminished concentration during a performance. Contrary to what some performers claim, Gould maintained that it was impossible to treat the audience as though they did not exist (Gould, undated, media script, "The Musical Life of the Future").

The listener was affected by a distracted performer in that a distortion of interpretation very often was the product of such an arrangement. Gould claimed that the performer was more concerned with things like trying to reach the marginal members of the audience than illuminating the structure of the music (Gould, undated, media script, "The Musical Life of the Future").

The ideal listener would, according to Gould, assume an ecstatic attitude that would be a shared, delicate thread binding the listener with the performer and composer in a web of inner awareness (Payzant, 1978). Gould contended that recording was the ideal medium for this to occur. Recordings seemed to impart certain advantages for the development of fuller and deeper listening experiences. These advantages include bypassing biographical data and concentrating on the musical art work, presenting the listener with multiple perspectives of a work, helping the performer to become closer to the listener, and making the listener the center of the performance problem.

The isolated listener of recordings could become involved in the music in such a way that extraneous biographical data, its preparation, its documentation, its performance, and postproduction processes would have little, if no, bearing on the listening experience (Gould, 1982c).

Recording could ideally present the listener with multiple perspectives of a work (Gould, 1983a). The listener could draw on these performance versions immediately.

The listener-performer relationship through the recording medium enables the performer to achieve an immediacy and closeness with the listener that is not possible in the live concert hall (Gould, 1980e). This can occur because of the isolated environment of the listener when hearing recordings. It is also the product of how the recordings are produced.

Finally, the listener rightly becomes the center of the performance problem (Gould, 1983a). The performer is not the focus, as is often in the live concert situation. The listener is given great importance since the musical concepts are focused on clear presentation.

INSTITUTIONS

By its very nature music appears to be transitory and artistic flux appears to be inevitable. As was cited in an earlier section, Gould wrote, "Every artist is in a state of flux or he wouldn't be an artist" (Gould, 1984b, p. 45). This seems to be unsettling for people and they attempt to give music some permanence by creating musical institutions.

Institutions provide an atmosphere in which a dialectical relationship between music's temporality and enduring features can exist (DaSilva et al., 1984). Institutions provide an habitual approach to conduct in order to influence a plurality of people (DaSilva et al., 1984). Gould (1966b) instinctively recognized the power of institutions and like several contemporary musical visionaries, commented critically on a number of musical institutions. He contended that the institutions that best represented us were those that were repositories of dissective opinion.

Music education. Gould was highly critical of prominent institutions of music education (e.g., Juilliard, Fontaine-bleau, and Tanglewood). He contended that these institutions kept the student in educational bondage and created several evils that the student had to overcome in order to achieve a satisfactory level of artistic freedom. The following are examples of how Gould (1984b) imagined students are kept in intellectual and artistic bondage.

Through a tutorial hierarchy, usually established by tenured faculty, the music student is bound to the major teacher with artistic umbilical ties that are virtually impossible to sever. The pupil is encouraged to remain bound to that teacher in subservience for a lifetime, never growing and experiencing real artistic and personal freedom. Obviously, Gould was opposed to the kind of relationship in which the teacher assumed a superior role and the student assumed an inferior role. He proposed that students should find their own way to personal truth and development. The teacher should merely help the student to focus on the student's own, already existing, artistic powers and musical vision. Students should be treated with deference and made aware of their self-worth.

Another quality promoted in traditional institutions of music education, which Gould speculated was undesirable, was the fact that students are treated like inferior entities by their professors. Gould proposed that ideal education occurred when the student and teacher were equal partners searching for the truth. He criticized what he believed to be the doctrinaire tactics of the neoprimitive idyllists of Tanglewood and the neoclassical strictures of Nadia Boulanger at Fontainebleau. Gould (1967b) called her pedagogic methods demagoguery. (It is curious that Gould accused Boulanger of demagoguery. Apparently, Gould had a superficial exposure to Nadia Boulanger's pedagogical philosophy and method. The hallmark of her teaching was her unbounded regard and enthusiasm for the individuality of her students.)

Gould (1984b) also disapproved of the indoctrination

that he said often occurs in learning institutions. He reasoned that learning takes place best when the student is drawn to ideas rather than brainwashed or indoctrinated.

Gould (1984b) judged that students should be active in their opinions and ideas. The student should not be passive to domineering teachers. Each person has a unique power to find personal solutions. The problem is to tap into it. Gould encouraged students to do this and to frame social constructs by which to govern themselves.

Lastly, Gould (1980b) was wary of the position of the performing artist made teacher in these musical institutions. He surmised that when a performing artist verbalized the processes that made things "work" there was a danger for the artist of becoming conscious of exactly what one was doing. When this occurred the performer might lose the proper mental relationship with that process. That in turn would inhibit spontaneity and the highest level of artistic expression. The "right-brained," nonverbal, spontaneous thinking state was important to Gould. This situation could be compared to love making. When we start thinking about how to maintain ourselves in the ecstatic milieu of love making, we lose it (Gallwey & Kriegel, 1977). When we think about how we perform, we lose it.

Competitions.   Gould was opposed to music competitions for a number of reasons. He argued that an individual's originality is discouraged at competitions. It is an irony at these competitions that some of the best musical talents are encouraged to preserve, in Gould's words, "a consensus of mediocrity—a mean line of temperamental indifference" (Gould, 1966e, pp. MA 23–24, 30). Competitions seem to favor the artist whose vision is less than ecstatic. Competitions seem to favor the artist who fails to attain the transcendental. Gould wrote,

> the notion of ecstasy as the only proper quest for the artist assumes competence as an inclusive component. The menace of the competitive idea is that through its emphasis upon consensus, it extracts that mean, indisputable, readily certifiable core of competence and leaves its eager, ill-

advised suppliants forever stunted, victims of a spiritual lobotomy. (Gould, 1966e, p. MA 30)

The test pieces used in competitions emphasize technical prowess rather than artistic vision. Gould maintained this was a deception in that the more important features of artistic expression are outweighed by showmanship and bravura (Gould, 1966e, p. MA 23–24, 30). The vocabulary used in connection with competitions is aggressive in tone. Expressions like "other bouts," "unpopular with the crowd," "the contestant triumphed," "the crowd was conquered," express a spirit of competitiveness and aggression that Gould disdained (Gould, 1974b, p. 77).

Finally, Gould found that juries used in competitions were inadequate to the task of judging. He thought they were musicians not especially qualified to judge or assess the artistic merits of their gifted contestants. Gould said that these juries were generally composed of musicians with careers of less than universal renown. Gould viewed these musicians as stunted practitioners who were not capable of affirming the mysteries of personality and temperament that are the pillars of re-creative vision (Gould, 1966e).

Because Gould claimed that competition does not improve the artist's disposition as a human being or as an artist, he offered the following suggestion to creatively circumvent competitive society and solve the problem of competition. He proposed that musical art should accept the alternatives offered by technology. Technology creates a protective shield for humanity and takes away the need for people to measure themselves with each other (Gould, 1978e). Technology could liberate us from sociological dynamics that detract from art's inner qualities.

The freedom to pursue an inner life has nothing to do with the physical setting that we find ourselves. Gould wrote,

I've never understood the preoccupation with freedom as its reckoned in the Western world. So far as I can see, freedom of movement usually has to do only with mobility,

and freedom of speech most frequently with socially
sanctioned verbal aggression and to be incarcerated would
be the perfect test of one's inner mobility and of the
strength which would enable one to opt creatively out of
the human situation. (Gould, 1974b, p. 78)

Indeed, Gould found (1978b) that artistic and personal
freedom are achieved and maintained through a personal
quest to discover and nurture one's inner life. For Gould
the ultimate attainment for imaginative "opter-outers" is
the acquisition and cultivation of a state of ecstasy.

Gould used the word "ecstasy" indiscriminately for a
quality of the music, a quality of the performer, an attitude
of the performer, and an attitude of the listener. Payzant
(1978) said that the essence of Gould's meaning of the
word "ecstasy" is a thread that joins together music,
performer, performance, and listener in a union of inner
awareness.

Critics. Gould criticized the critics as being an institution, a bulwark of traditional culture and values. Because
the critics defended either implicitly or explicitly the
framework of a traditional music society, Gould viewed
them with artistic suspicion. He thought that the critic who
serves as aesthetic arbiter has no real social function or
defensible criteria on which to base subjective judgments.
Depending on the nature of the society in which the critic
serves, Gould said that "one might make a case for the critic
as propagandist" (Gould, 1984b, p. 257).

Gould (1977c) also suggested that we could redefine the
critic's role as consumer-advocate. The critic might then be
retrained to function as a data collector who is confined to
objective comment making. Therefore, the critic would no
longer be a morally disruptive and aesthetically destructive
influence.

IDEAS FOR A THEORY OF MUSIC

What is a theory of music? Lerdahl and Jackendoff (1983)
proposed that a theory of music consists of principles that

underlie an analytical system. It is a formal description of musical intuitions that are experienced and drawn from musical expression. They suggested that an analytical method is valuable especially when it enables one to articulate insights into music compositions.

Gould's theoretical construct of ideas for a music theory consists of the following components: forming materials, musical processes, psychology of a music theory, and analysis/syntax.

Forming Materials

Forming materials (Lippman, 1977) are essential features of the intrinsic nature of music. Gould assigned great importance to two forming materials: structure/architecture, and harmony.

STRUCTURE/ARCHITECTURE

We can ascertain that Gould (1962c) considered the structure/architecture of music to be very important by the fact that he stressed these qualities in his writings about music. What did Gould mean by the idea of a structure/architecture? In spite of the fact that Gould suggested that structure should be a strong concept in one's relationship to music, he did not offer an explicit definition of structure in his writings. Instead, he offered clues to assist our interpretation of exactly what he meant by structure/architecture. He offered criteria that help us piece together a greater understanding of this concept. The following is a presentation of these characteristics.

Structure should act as a governing principle by which the composer, performer, and listener comprehend music. This governing principle acts as an approach or method that defines the parameters by which we understand and present music. Thus, the principle of structure ought to be foremost in one's technique and should permeate the composition in several musical dimensions (Cott, 1984).

Structure could be thought of as a relative quality that

changes according to the analytical system that one employs (Cott, 1984). Thus, one creates the kind of structure one employs by the system one uses in analysis. Gould believed that, as a performer, one could possibly use different analytical systems, at various times, in order to gain disparate insights concerning a musical art work. Using different analytical systems was a kind of composing in that the performer could emphasize or detract from certain features of the composition. The performer could reshape the stuff of composition, and thus, by employing a particular structural model, share a kind of multiple authorship with the composer. As was demonstrated earlier, Gould supported multiple authorship. And, his belief in multiple authorship helped him to justify the basis for his highly experimental and controversial performance practice.

Gould (1984b) considered cohesion and stability to be notable features of structure. In a description of Paul Hindemith's compositional method, Gould (1984b) mentioned that structural cohesion was a focal point in Hindemith's aesthetic intent. By his comments, Gould implied that structural cohesion was a desirable trait of the compositional process.

Structures can be static, that is, formally predictable, or dynamic. In comments about J. S. Bach's aesthetic, Gould said that Bach was an example of a composer whose structures of music were dynamic and fluid. For Bach, no part of the structure is more important. Rather, the perpetual motion and endless flow of the structure are the dominating factors (Gould, 1961). Gould offered additional insight into differences of static and dynamic structure and wrote,

> In Bach's music there is no sense of the formally predictable, and generations of music listeners raised in the expectation of static events marking the main structural divisions of art have often misunderstood the shape, the structure, the message of Bach. In Bach, almost every work must be allowed to present to us an architectural shape

which does not conform to any other that we know, but which is responsible to itself only. (Gould, 1961, pp. 6–7)

Gould (1979c) implied that structure was more elemental or basic than instrumentation. Instrumentation was considered peripheral to the structure or backbone of the piece. Gould used Bach, again, as an example of a composer who also felt this way. He said that Bach was too involved with structure to be overly concerned with instrumentation. Indeed, Bach interchanged instrumentation for a number of works (e.g., *Violin Concerto in E Major* was reset for the keyboard in D Major). Gould did not believe that structure and sonority were complementary aspects of the artistic work. Rather, he concentrated his main attention on structure considering sonority peripheral (Youngren, 1983).

As was previously mentioned, Gould declared that structure could be justifiably tempered by the performer. This could be accomplished by changes within a tempo. Gould asserted that the tempo the performer chooses creates, within that tempo field, a certain level of tensions and relationships. These relationships are, in a manner of speaking, contained within the chosen tempo. And, the fact that one might choose a fast or slow tempo has no bearing on the structure or emotional content of a composition (Cott, 1984). Gould thought tempo was more a function of extraneous factors (e.g., the piano, or the hall) than structure.

Gould cited Artur Schnabel as an example of a performer who created a strong sense of structure through the use of pulse and paragraph in chosen tempi. Gould wrote, "I'm very aware of constant pulse—Schnabel was aware of the pulse of the paragraph. He was certainly aware of the interior pulse as well, but he chose to let it ride through the paragraph, as if he were dictating a letter with a certain series of commas and semicolons . . ." (Cott, 1984, pp. 60–61).

Finally, Gould considered a well-defined bass line in

performance to be seminal to his conception of the structure of the music (Cott, 1984).

HARMONY

The harmonic basis for music is the diatonic relationships each member of the harmonic "solar system" has with each other. This dynamic interrelationship changes according to the musical style and the era in which a musical composition is framed. A chord's relative importance to the tonic is achieved according to the structural concepts outlined by the composer. Tonality has less to do with triads than with the ideas that bind them together (Gould, 1957, 1958b, 1967a).

Gould offered two examples of the use of triads. (1) In classical tonality, there is a subtle gradation of modulation (Gould, 1957, 1958b). The modulation is not sudden but gradual and finely tuned. This is key-centered tonality with all of its inherent, well-known progressions. (2) The extension of the Wagnerian modulation achieved by Arnold Schoenberg used triads outside of tonality. Modulatory ambiguities were employed (Gould, 1979a). Schoenberg enacted the final break with key-centered harmony by using triadic forms in a systematic serialization (Gould, 1962h). In describing this process, Gould wrote, it is "an idea of harmony within serialism that might be more accurately described as a vocabulary of triadic relationship beyond the scope of key-centered tonality" (Gould, 1967a). Triads existed but were entities which did not confirm or deny the key-centered tonality they suggested. This was tonality weakened in its last stages (Gould, 1964b, p. 5). This was harmony within serialism (Gould, 1967a).

Throughout his writings about music, Gould (1981) centered on harmonic considerations. Harmonic variety was considered a criterion for great music. He contended that harmony was also a very important basis for arriving at structural concepts in analysis. Thus, when he described various historical practices, he described them in the light of harmonic dynamics. An example of such writing is Gould's citation of Alban Berg's ability to transcend the limits of key relationships by various techniques. Berg "tried to punctuate (perhaps to cadentialize?) . . . with latent pauses and apostrophes," and he achieved "pseudoharmonic emphasis with octave doublings" (Gould, 1958a). Gould called Berg's work the last example of tonality betrayed (Gould, 1958a).

Concerning harmonic function and the inversion of the triad, Gould did not agree that an inversion of a triad was still that triad in its primary function. He wrote, "I don't believe in that at all—but in the sense that you could have a certain cluster and there would be one note absent from it that was the key to its function as a cluster, the key to where it was going and point from which it had come" (Cott, 1984, p. 53). Gould cited the opening of Wagner's Tristan as an example of this procedure. Schoenberg, according to Gould, based his whole analytical precepts on the notion of the absent-root (Cott, 1984). Gould wrote of Schoenberg's process, ". . . any conceivable configurational plan, so long as it remained faithful to a root, present or absent or whatever, was viable and made the situation admissible" (Gould, 1984b, p. 53).

MUSICAL PROCESSES

Musical processes are the procedures, the systematic actions used and directed toward a musical end. Four of the musical processes Gould commented on in his writings are presented here: fugue, contrapuntal invention, tone row and motivic development, and variation.

FUGUE

According to Gould (1972, 1969e), fugue is more than a form. It is a process which causes changes in form according to the idiosyncratic requirements of a particular musical composition. The successful composer of fugue must relinquish formulae aimed at creating form and flexibly adapt the music to the requirements set by the fugal process. Thus, a fugue is a dialogue which changes according to its setting. Gould wrote, "There is, to the composer, the enormous satisfaction of dealing with a musical form in which the form *itself* becomes the servant of a subjectively manipulated concept of thematic relation" (Gould, 1964h, p. 54).

Fugal process represents most the concept of unceasing motion. But in spite of this, fugue is concerned with relatively confined areas of musical expanse. It is mainly concerned with intense subjective concentration on the details of the moment. Fugue is not involved with broad aspects of dramatic altercation or elaborate shifts of texture or dynamics. It is involved with the manipulation of semiautonomous musical ideas in pattern. Gould explained the process further: "Among these patterns, the effect of textural variety is fostered by a sensation of pregnant pause within one or other of the contributing voices" (Gould, 1964h, p. 53).

The fugue, when considered as a form, is really a combination of Renaissance techniques of imitation and voice-leading, and baroque concepts of key-order and harmonic progression (Gould, 1979c). Gould wrote, "All of the effects of fugue (except that of the vertical gravitation of key and key contrast) were effects formulated in the early years of the Renaissance—in the generation before the tonal grammar of tension and relaxation had been made articulate" (Gould, 1964h, p. 50).

Gould (1964h) found the fugal process to be a shield from the pressures of musical fashion. He called the fugue one of the most lasting creative devices in music history. It has outlived musical eras right to modern times. Perhaps it has done so because it can arouse in the listener a kind of primeval curiosity that, examines the rise and fall, the call and the echo, the statement and answer found in primeval imaginations that predate modern aesthetic molding (Gould, 1964h).

Because fugue is a fluid process, in ages of reason the fugue appears to be unreasonable (Gould, 1972, 1975g). Fugue is ultimately about the techniques at the composer's disposal and making something of it that is otherworldly.

CONTRAPUNTAL INVENTION

Gould (1958a) implied in his writing that the contrapuntal process is an ongoing process less important for what it is than for what it can become. Contrapuntal techniques are in sharp contrast with other musical techniques because they emphasize ongoing process rather than stability. He wrote in explanation, "This indeed is the fundamental distinction between this sort of compositional technique (counterpoint) and that in which the melodic line (no matter how organically concerned) is given importance per se" (Gould, 1958a). Gould seemed to favor such a fluid, indeterminate approach towards music. He considered contrapuntal invention a criterion, along with harmonic and rhythmic variety, for a musical composition to be evaluated as great music.

Gould's (1977b) frequent reference to counterpoint in his writings indicates that contrapuntal invention had high priority in his musical aesthetics (e.g., Gould's reference to counterpoint in his essay on Sibelius). In his essay about Schoenberg's string sextet, *Verklärte Nacht,* Gould placed great emphasis on inner voice structure, the bass line, and the counterpoint (Gould, 1962h).

Gould (1980e) went so far as to say that he was not interested in music that did not offer a contrapuntal design. By this he did not mean counterpoint in the sense of formal fugue writing but the contrapuntal process. For Gould, that process combined and totally integrated the vertical as well as horizontal musical material. When contrapuntal textures were not readily apparent in compositions Gould performed, he would invent contrapuntal implications in his performances. One example of this is his infamous performance of Mozart's *Concerto K. 491.* In this performance he supplied contrapuntal passages that Mozart did not pen (Haggin, 1984).

Contrapuntal music interested Gould (1982d) because, in his own words, it is music with an explosion of simultaneous ideas. It is music where the quality of ideas are implied. The concept of an equality of musical ideas emanated from the Renaissance aesthetic and interested

Gould. Musical equality could be described as a metaphor for spiritual equality in Gould's morally inspired aesthetics.

TONE ROW AND MOTIVIC DEVELOPMENT

Gould (1953) offered the following interpretation of tone row. He said that the tone row should not be considered a scale. A scale functions as a kind of reference catalog of tones for a composition. A tone row implies more. The tone row serves as a characteristic pattern for the composition. It combines independent motives into melodic prototypes. These melodic prototypes are small nuclei of musical activity that participate on all the levels of a composition. Schoenberg's obsession with this compositional process is an example of its use (Gould, undated, T.V. script, "Anthology of Variation").

Tone rows are often contrived in order to demonstrate motivic combinations that limit rather than increase the material of the composition (Gould, 1958a). Gould saw motives as elements of a musical process in which these units were ultimately phased out. Gould cited Hindemith's music as an example of this process put into practice and wrote,

> He [Hindemith] lacks some ultimate, transformational impulse—the willingness, perhaps, to set aside the burden of motivic development—the very quality through which, as so often in the final measures of a Wagner opera or a Strauss tone poem, the motivic strands themselves are ultimately dematerialized. (Gould, 1978a)

VARIATION

All music is about other music and is possible because of other music. In this sense all music is a variation on some other music. This statement was central in Gould's view of the variation principle. Gould's notion of variation was that variation was all-encompassing. He extended the concept's parameters, to conclude with Schoenberg, that all music is also philosophically variative (Gould, undated, T.V. script, "Anthology of Variation").

How is music philosophically variative? Gould explained that our concepts of variation are nothing more than our concepts for society. These concepts are based on a progressive view of history. They are based on the thought that our quest for knowledge and discovery is a search for the future. Our actions are grounded in a referential background that consists of the productivity of all former generations, and these views of historical progressivism are reflected in art (Gould, undated, T.V. script, "Anthology of Variation").

The variative principle, as described by Gould, was a dialectic between the progressivism of occidental culture and the retrogressions of primitive societies. Gould claimed that primitive cultures did not share with modern cultures the linear, progressive attitude of culture. Rather, primitive societies searched for moments of revelation, moments in which humanity's destiny was clearly defined. Gould wrote that these cultures cultivate a spiritual attitude that encourages each generation to ponder the moment on which the gods of transcendence intervened in the life of the culture. The culture then develops artistic symbols that attempt to mystically recall the power of that intervention (Gould, undated, T.V. script, "Anthology of Variation").

Gould maintained that at the root of the concept of variation was a tension between the two polarities of progressivism and its inverse, retrogression (Gould, undated, T.V. script, "Anthology of Variation").

Finally, Gould said that the contemporary conception of variation was influenced by psychoanalysis. It has begun to examine the relationship of chance to purpose and the conditions of creativity in the shadow of its antithetical position—negativity. It has also considered musical structure in relation to a superstructure of silence (Gould, undated, T.V. script, "Anthology of Variation").

Clearly, Gould framed his insights of the variation principle with a psychology of a music theory in mind.

PSYCHOLOGY OF A MUSIC THEORY

Lerdahl and Jackendoff (1983) wrote that the understanding of musical cognition is a psychological phenomenon. Gould's ideas concur with them and Arnheim (1967) that apprehension of the musical reality is more than a recording of sensory elements. It is the framing of human qualities and intuitions. It is within this context that Gould implied a rich source of hypotheses concerning psychological musical universals.

Gould (1956e, 1960) attributed a psychological dimension to musical compositions. He supported analysis based on the psychological dimensions inherent in the music. Gould often engaged in analyzing and describing music's dynamics by making use of psychological references. Examples of this kind of activity include Gould's (1979a) reference to psychological dynamics in Schoenberg's *Piano Concerto, Opus 42*, and the concerto idea depicted by Gould (1984b) as being a psychological tension between aggression and reluctance, power and pleading.

Gould (1984b) imagined that every observable phenomenon has its own concealed psychological shadow. And, therefore, if one were to aptly penetrate musical meaning one would relate one's intuitions through a psychologically meaningful vocabulary. One might relate the objective phenomenon and the consequent psychological response that it presupposes. This implies the presence of a theory of musical expression.

Certain musical devices are embedded within the psychological consciousness of modern culture. They include the following concepts: statement and answer, or subject and response (Gould, 1964h); setting up distant harmonic relationships with conjunctive harmonies, then removing the conjunctive material. The result leaves one psychologically with only reminiscences of the intercessionary material and exposes the most distant related polarities to each other (Gould, 1967a); emphasis of the melodic line versus the contrapuntal concept of psychological equality for the voices (Gould, 1958a); in some circles, especially of the nineteenth century, the root of a chord was thought to be psychologically perceptible, but not necessarily physically present. Gould did not agree with the theory that proposed you do not have to sound a root for that tone to be psychologically present (Cott, 1984).

When a composition is successful, its rhetorical demands are transcended by a simultaneously personal and universal affirmation (Gould, 1984b). But compositions should be devoid of egoistic pomposity. There may be psychological reasons why a compositional style may be appealing. In the list of reasons that Gould provided for why Mahler's music was successful, the following psychological reasons were presented. Mahler delighted in mixing the sublime with the inane. Mahler attempted to synopsize and transcend all experience through art. Mahler put unusual musical and psychological demands on the listener (Gould, 1974a).

Gould (1971) reasoned that somehow music was the product of a composer's psyche, spiritual or psychological status. An example of this is what he wrote of Mahler: "Mahler's symphonies are above all, the creation of a disturbed and dissatisfied man" (Gould, 1953). The personal temperament of the composer modifies the composer's creative output.

Another dimension of the psychology of music theory is the psychology of improvisation. Gould framed the following features of a psychology of improvisation: The more interesting aspect of improvisation is the way that it relates to notated music; The relationship between the organized and the spontaneous structure rests on the preconceptions we possess in our analysis of them; When improvising the musician cannot be as thoughtful about the arrangement of the musical material because of psychological duress (Gould, 1966c).

The psychological assumption that a composer's work is the direct result of conscious industry is often made by nonmusicians. People seem to instinctively look for signs of premonition in musical creativity. Gould wrote, " . . . we try to convince ourselves that we're not simply involved in an errant, sensual experience." Gould asked the question, how many of our thoughts derive from conscious industry or from concealed, unacknowledged desires? Gould was concerned with the fact that the nonmusician thought that the composer must know a score more as a logician would than in an intuitive way. Gould held that this attitude should be held suspect and watched (Gould, 1966c).

Finally, Gould (1953, 1956a) proposed that the gratification of the mind and of the senses is not separable in art. The whole person is involved in the musical experience, whether it be as composer, performer, or listener. Thus, a psychology of music theory plays an important part, since music involves the whole person, in clarifying and making meaningful that theory.

ANALYSIS/SYNTAX

The analysis of a musical composition includes discussions of syntax. Syntax gives meaning to the tones, how they relate to each other, in a congeneric context. Gould (1962h) placed great emphasis on an analysis/syntax that discovered structure and contrapuntal elements in a composition. Gould concluded that very often these features were implicit and not necessarily explicit in a composition. His controversial performance practice of finding inner voices and structural relationships that were not readily apparent was based on this premise.

Furthermore, a system of analysis should fit the composition being analyzed. Gould wrote, "There is nothing so futile as the attempt to make a work of art serve a system of analysis for the conformation of which it was not created" (Gould, 1967a). An example of a system analysis that could be used in a number of situations was Schoenberg's method to reduce all sound to the lowest possible denominator. This was a system which surveyed a musical composition for motivic elements that could be considered embryonic in the piece's development. Gould (1953) wrote that the evolution of this approach in analysis coincided with the decline of tonality. It replaced the architectural function of the decaying harmonic language. Audiences that were bored with predictable harmonic practices were confronted with a musical syntax in which ambiguity was all.

Gould (1959b) favored the use of an instinctive logic in analyzing music rather than a mathematical model. He said that mathematical analysis was extramusical, a too-artificial paradigm and not an appropriate vehicle for the analytical process in music. Gould asserted in his writings that analysis should be grounded in the music, not in external systems. Instinctive logic is grounded in and emanates from the musical composition. It is, therefore, a good basis for analysis.

Finally, Gould (1966c) warned that trying to objectify music in analysis would prove to be a futile exercise. In the end, music is really about nothing in particular and allows great latitude for various interpretations.

IDEAS FOR A THEORY OF MUSIC CRITICISM

Gould (1956e) agreed with George Bernard Shaw that parsing is not the business of criticism. Criticism should encompass more ideas than merely discussions of syntactical relationships.

VALUES AS CRITERIA FOR EVALUATING ART

Gould (1956a) proposed in his writings the following values as criteria for the music critic. (1) Critics should judge composers and performers on the basis of whether exhibitionism exists in their art. Gould maintained that exhibitionism detracts from the real issues of art and should be eliminated in art (Gould, undated, media script, "Artist as Artisan"). (2) Composers can be categorized according to their interest or lack of interest in instrumental sonority (e.g., Bartók was interested in instrumental sonority; Bach was not) (Gould, 1975f). (3) Music should not be judged on the basis of historical data. Gould agreed with Albert Schweitzer that human thought is at its strongest when it is not concerned with historical circumstances.

(4) Musical values are relative and not absolute. It has been demonstrated in music history that values change with time (Gould, 1974c). Therefore, the music critic must

be flexible in forming opinions. It should be noted that the problem of an analytical double standard, as a critical issue, could become involved. For example, is a composer's technique the result of poor craftsmanship or is the composer aiming at a predetermined value beyond craft and the composing process? (5) Music should not be evaluated on the basis of whether it is original or not. It is often assumed that if a composer demonstrates originality in a composition then the composition is more valuable. Gould (1964b) questioned the presence of originality in art as an indication that a work is more valuable.

If a compositional value, like unity, happens to be out of fashion, then the composer who employs such a value is considered out of fashion. Gould (1964f) cited Mendelssohn as an example of a composer whose stylistic gestures conceal a moving, puritanical quality that was considered outmoded for his time because it did not conform to the prevalent aesthetic standard. Gould argued that our ideas about whether an artistic procedure is appropriate or not emanate from our notion that history is a series of climaxes. Artists are evaluated according to how much they participate in the historical fluctuations and climax.

Other aesthetic values that Gould (1970b) thought were important for the consideration of music criticism are as follows: A composer should reflect a passionate but antisensual nature in art; Compositions should demonstrate spontaneity and objective discipline (Gould, 1956b); Composers should mirror a contemplative, nonaggressive personality in their art; There is no necessity for the performer to differentiate between tactile and intellectual considerations (Gould, 1972); Critics should be aware of the use of silence in music. They should understand the important use of pauses in the texture as an integral part of the texture (Gould, 1971c).

THE ELECTRONIC AGE AND MUSIC CRITICISM

Critics should be conscious of the fact that the electronic age has changed musical values. This has happened in the following ways. Terms used for music (i.e., imitation, invention, originality) no longer connote the precise, analytical concepts they once represented; Electronic transmission has inspired new modes of creativity like multilevel participation in creativity (Gould, 1964a); Twentieth-century compositional thinking, which is inspired by electronic techniques, has influenced the performance practice of premodern music (Gould, 1976e); Art is not technology, and therefore, cannot be judged by standards set for technology. Differences that occur among composers cannot be compared to the differences that may occur in technical equipment. When one functions as a critic, one should not try to totally objectify musical art works (Gould, 1962a).

CHRONOLOGY AND MUSIC CRITICISM

Gould (1961, 1965g) was opposed to the notion that the particular chronology connected with a musical art work somehow influenced the quality of that art work. Gould believed that dependence on the concept of chronological progression was a limiting factor. He claimed there are times in art when what is thought of as retrogression may instead be progression in an art work's dynamics. A composer may totally work outside of the expected chronology. Gould presented Bach as an example of such a composer who seemed to work outside the passage of time. Gould also cited Charles Ives as a composer who did not bother with precedence and consequence or his historical role.

Gould (1964f) thought that Western criticism tends to greatly exaggerate the concept of historical transformation. Such criticism was too infected with extraneous ideas about progress. He reacted to the chronological progress versus retrogression theory by rejecting it. Gould was suspect of the so-called artistic chronological parallel and believed most claims of artistic judgment derive from an "art-for-what-its-society-was-once-like" sake rather than the more desired "art-for-art's-sake" approach. He also wrote that participation in a certain historical movement does not always impose upon the participant the duty to accept the logical implications of that movement.

Gould (1962a) addressed the issue of critics using longevity as a standard to judge or measure creative life. He concluded that this is possible only if longevity measures the development of the composer as a human being. It is evident that Gould's ideas for a theory of music criticism appear to be grounded in a humanistic philosophy.

Finally, the following questions were framed by Gould (1984b) concerning how one might interpret musical art within a chronology. What is it that really provides the influence of one generation upon another? Is it simply the retention of stylistic similarities within an ever-moving historical front? Or can it not also be the inspiration to be drawn from a life which contains a total achievement of art?

INVENTION AND MUSIC CRITICISM

Gould (1965b) separated invention from greatness in music. He believed that invention was simply the stepping aside from normal expectations and did not imply automatic greatness in a composition. Music that was inventive had to be critically assessed on the basis of other inherent qualities and values.

The concept of invention presupposes that one adheres to premises different than those expected. This could occur in composition as well as performance. Gould (1980b) implied in his writings that the following questions could be used as a basis for evaluating invention in performance:

1) Does the performance explore the possibility of different registrations in the composition (e.g., playing the piano but thinking of orchestral timbres)?
2) Does the performance project the music as being in linear voices rather than vertical blocks? Does the

performance clarify the structure by illuminating contrapuntal implications in the music?

3) Does the performance use a phrasing system that comes from another musical medium? As an example, Gould related the account of when he edited piano music for a recording and imagined that the phrasing involved was of a bowed system.

4) Does the performance imply that a different sound system was in the back of the composer's mind? If so, what was that sound system? Gould wrote that most renowned composers for the piano have written for that instrument with another sound system in mind. He believed sometimes this has worked and sometimes it has not (e.g., the use of the post-Wagnerian orchestra sound system for piano works has dismally failed).

5) Does the performance incorporate unexpected articulations? Gould (1980b) was opposed to the "grand tradition" of legato in piano playing and proposed that detached articulation was more inventive.

6) What is the performer's use of rubato? Does it illuminate the music's structure? The critic should recognize the points raised in these questions and evaluate according to the implied premises.

How Should the Critic Consider Art?

It is implied in Gould's writings that we should create, recreate, and interpret art with a mind-set that transcends the dogmatic conventions of the art world. He concluded that the dogmatizations of art were, in his words, "the frivolous, effete preoccupations of the chronologists" (Gould, 1984b, p. 92). One such biased fashion concerns value judgments in art and how they relate to an awareness of identity. Critics often hesitate in making judgments about an art work when they are unaware of the identity of the creator. Gould proposed that the critic should not be concerned with the lack of identity but offer aesthetic judgments based on the work itself (Cott, 1984).

Gould proposed that we should bypass the outmoded, worn-out preoccupations of aesthetics and adopt an attitude of uncompromising individuality towards art that ignores conformity for conformity's sake. This brand of individuality was aptly described by Gould when he wrote,

> It is an ultimate argument of individuality—an argument of the innateness of individual effort, be it self-willed or predetermined, be it logical or be it mystic—an argument that man can create his own synthesis of time without being bound by the conformities that time imposes. (Gould, 1961)

When we escape from the creative and re-creative conventions of culture, we can be open to an infinite variety of musical systems. When we ignore conventional rhetoric we are in a position to transcend its limitations. Our capability and capacity for individuality is greatly expanded (Gould, 1968c). Thus, the critic can view art with decided openness.

MUSIC CRITICISM AND PERFORMANCE

Critics may be at a loss for a yardstick to evaluate musical performances. Gould (1973c) constructed a model of mock criteria that epitomizes the contradictory comments critics sometimes make and doubts criticism's underlying tenets. Critics can (1) enthusiastically accept a performance as fresh, free from tradition (a collection of bad habits); (2) doubt the validity of an interpretation by saying that the performance has not jelled or it is an interpretation in search of an architectural overview; or (3) "straddle the fence" and make one's criticism a combination of numbers (1) and (2).

What should a critic's normative paradigm, used to judge legitimate musical interpretations, contain? The following is a list of points Gould (1976e) indicated were important for the critic of musical performance to consider:

1) The critic might look for cliché-ridden elements in a performance. Cliché should be avoided in a good performance and the critic can judge accordingly;

2) The critic should look for a feeling of direction in the musical performance. The performance should indicate a sense that each note fits within a structure (Gould, 1980b);

3) The pace of the performance should be contingent upon the harmonic routine and structure. Change of tempi should not overemphasize thematic elements when they are the result of customary harmonic progression and modulation (Gould, 1980e).

In regard to a masculine/feminine approach to pacing in Mozart's piano sonatas, Gould argued that because Mozart did not emphasize the inherent crystallization of opposite forces in the development section, then one should not change tempo with a change of key or theme. One should play these sonatas in a straightforward manner (Cott, 1984);

4) The critic should discount the unrealistic performance practices of contemporary baroque specialists. A new glossary of superimposed notions can work equally well (Gould, 1968c);

5) The critic should avoid the belief that turn-of-the-century performance practice represented a kind of summit in performance tradition. He or she should be open to a variety of practices (Gould, 1974c);

6) The critic should be interested in the crystallization of the physical and spiritual through artistic expression. There should be a oneness of art and artist expressed by complete subjectivity in performance (Gould, 1953).

MUSIC CRITICISM AND COMPOSITION

Gould (1974c) indicated in his writings the following would be helpful to the music critic in assessing compositions:

1) Good writing lets the listener use imagination to flesh out the material of the composition;

2) A composition can be effective in spite of the extensive use of formulae. Gould (1968a) cited the keyboard works of Domenico Scarlatti as examples of this type of writing;

3) The composer does not have to develop ideas in an extensive, discursive way in order to be effective and convincing. A composer's work can be appealing in simplicity (Gould, 1968a);

4) Everything of consequence in music composition does not have to possess a strong zeitgeist coloration. Composers can be successful in drawing inspiration from other aesthetics (Gould, 1980b);

5) The critic should avoid the attitude that "novelty equals progress equals great art" in a musical composition. It is essential to acquire a more flexible system of values for music criticism (Gould, 1964b, p. 2);

6) The same subjectivity achieved by performer and work in performance can also be manifest in art works. Gould (1953) mentions Alban Berg and James Joyce as examples of creators who achieved total subjectivity;

7) Critics should employ criteria in their analysis that will recognize and explore the relationship between music and metaphysics. Gould considered this the "realm of technical transcendence" (Gould, 1956f). The critic should recognize the vision of subconscious design in music grounded in intuitive perception.

IDEAS FOR AN EPISTEMOLOGY OF MUSIC

There has been a strong tendency to try to limit the field of knowledge to only those forms that can be verified in special ways (Reid, 1941). This perspective has been shaped mostly by positivism and its objectivist framework. But authors like Reese (1980) and Bowman (1982) have offered an alternative vision that assents to the statement that, "We know more than we can tell" (Polanyi, 1962).

Ideas from Gould's writings profess a similar viewpoint

of the field of knowledge. His observations concerning art are rooted in a humanistic standard far from positivistic perception. They include an openness, a willingness to seek and experience other kinds of knowing (e.g., knowledge of a subjective character, the knowledge of transcendence).

Gould persistently related aesthetic matters to other cognitive enterprises, including ideas for the development of an epistemology of music. He implicitly studied and analytically explored points like the following: What kinds of knowledge does music reveal? What are the conditions that promote knowing a work of musical art? What is the relationship of the performer to musical knowledge? What is the relationship of knowledge and music pedagogy? These issues and their subsequent explorations helped frame Gould's opinion of a musical knowledge.

WHAT KINDS OF KNOWLEDGE DOES MUSIC REVEAL?

Gould (1980b) professed that music is a kind of conduit for personal revelation. Through music we can better know what is revealed. True revelation comes from one's observation of oneself and not outside forces. Revelation is the answer that emanates from within oneself.

Gould is not clear as to the exact meaning and full import of the concept of revelation. We only know that he thought revelation is possible and that it comes in the form of an answer from within. Is it an answer for performance problems? Is it an answer concerning psychological growth factors? Do the answers of revelation give us unique, personal, artistic knowledge unobtainable elsewhere?

Music discloses the knowledge of a subjective, personal inspiration. In the moment that we make music, we can know this inner inspiration. It is then, rather than in plotted times, that it is possible to know the inspiration of openness to spontaneous structural expansion within the music. It is at that moment that inspiration is the supreme test of our entire persona (Gould, 1958a).

Through music we can know a system of emotional

reference. But there are times when composers like Arnold
Schoenberg use a language that has no generally accepted
reference. Although that reference is vague and unfamiliar it still has the power to manifest emotional knowledge
(Gould, 1964b).

Music has apparent allegorical or metaphorical connotations, especially in the highest sense of a metaphysics.
Gould (1964b) said that music is also a means of expressing
communication's mysteries in an equally mysterious form.

CONTRAPUNTAL IMAGERY

Gould used the metaphor of contrapuntal imagery in
much of his creative work and life attitudes. Contrapuntal
thought is evident in his performances, compositions, and
media projects. Throughout his writings he demonstrated
that music reveals through contrapuntal imagery a metaphor for a vision of life. This vision was rooted in moral
and social principles.

To think contrapuntally means to synthesize complex
events into a unifying vision. Making simple the complex is
a way of knowing and comprehending reality. Contrapuntal thinking obliterates the dialectics of historical chronology. In contrapuntal textures every note has a past and a
future that undermines chronological thinking. It is also a
metaphor for an awareness of a life of the spirit. Through
this epistemological perspective, a fresh look at musical
knowing is presented. This new idea portrays music as a
model for our comprehension of life's dynamics.

WHAT ARE THE CONDITIONS THAT FACILITATE KNOWING A WORK OF MUSICAL ART?

Music discloses itself. Gould (1964b, 1956b) framed a list of
conditions for music to better unfold:

1) We should not use historical chronology as a basis to
   criticize and understand a work of musical art. Gould

maintained that one should go to the work itself for deeper knowledge. Any external factors are superficial to the art work's main import.

2) It is dangerous to interpret art, and then, through philosophical connotation, accept this interpretation (paraphrase) as a valid depiction of the author's intellectual attitude. It is false to base musical judgments on philosophical conjecture rather than on immediate musical analysis. This is another example of going to the art work for knowledge.

3) We cannot know music by studying a composer's life. It is a misconception to attribute characteristics and dimensions of a composer's private life as direct influences on musical consciousness.

How Do We Learn (Know) Music?

We can discover how we learn to know music by first recognizing that all of our learning is grounded in our exposure to other experiences. Our immediate experiences are bound to other related experiences and we tend to evaluate our knowledge in terms of these adjacent experiences (Gould, 1968c). On a wider scale Gould claimed that an intellectual climate or posture could be conditioned by past concepts. He wrote, " . . . the intellectual posture of our time was incontestably conditioned by the post-Romantic concept of free association, the influence of the subconscious, and the starry delusion that the great artist lives for great moments" (Gould, 1960b, p. 76).

It is through ecstatic musical experiences that we learn and know beyond the surface of momentary musical expressions. Through this kind of personal knowledge, we are able to probe into deeper levels of artistic and transcendent consciousness (Gould, 1973c). Music reveals itself on multilevel consciousness. Gould highly valued this subjective form of knowing a musical work.

We can learn music through listening to musical clichés. Musical clichés come to us in many ways, but, predominately through background music. Gould indicated that we learn musical clichés subliminally when background music is played. This affects our musical language by broadening our base of musical ideas. When this occurs, we also appear to accept dissonant devices as fully understandable (Gould, 1964b). Gould did not explore how this process transforms our learning. But he persistently favored the omnipresence of music in our lives through the controversial Muzakian environment. He wrote that he could not understand why people get upset over Muzak. Gould claimed he could listen to insipid music and never be bothered by it (Gould, 1964b).

Gould could make such a statement because he strongly believed in the cliché form of musical presentation as a force that would transform the musical vocabulary of our popular culture. He thought that if people heard music, even in cliché form, they would develop a base by which they could put serious music in relief. He tried to legitimatize the constant background music in the environment of our culture.

We learn music through personal revelation. Gould (1965b) insinuated that other forms of knowledge can be subject to revelation. As an example he wrote that very often students confound their teachers with revelatory insights that turn a jaded masterpiece into a fresh, new experience. Their professors, who do not consider art subject to revelation, condemn the student's insights.

Learning occurs in subtle ways and students do best when drawn to ideas rather than brainwashed or indoctrinated mindlessly. Gould (1984b) argued that ideal education occurs when the student and teacher are equal participants in a quest for the truth. He held that students should be active in voicing their opinions. They should not be passive to dominating teachers but should develop qualities of self-reliance and self-sufficiency in their musical and educational life.

Gould (1964b) questioned how we know music. Is music based on logic? Or is it the result of unexplainable factors? Gould concurred with the latter position that art is a mystery and cannot be completely objectified. This was the quality in art that gave it its elusive and unpredictable power.

Gould claimed that no system, no matter how highly developed, can do more than put into practice the elusive qualities of good judgment and taste in the practitioner (Gould, 1964b). Can a practitioner know the basis for taste and good judgment? Gould proposed several insightful criteria for the development of good taste.

Gould (1984b) stressed that knowledge is blocked by gratuitous advice on the part of the teacher. He wrote that the separateness of individual experience limits the usefulness of any practical advice given. He believed that the uniqueness of each person's experience cannot transcend the barriers of communication because the unknown is always present. Universals cannot be fabricated from individual experience. Rather, each artist should find a unique, personal way to truth and development.

We can also know a musical work in a psychological way. Gould claimed that the listener could be involved in a kind of psychological comprehension; the listener focuses on psychological factors in the music. Gould cited Schoenberg as an example of a composer who inspires greater psychological involvement on the part of the listener (Gould, 1962g). In addition, sometimes people view a composer's work as a reflection of the composer's state of psychological mind (Gould, 1967a).

We also know music through our imagination. The "inner ear of the imagination is very much more powerful a stimulant than is any amount of outward observation" (Gould, 1984c, p. 7). Gould exhorts us to be deeply involved with the process of our imaginations. Ideally, this imagination is not an alternative to what seems to be the reality of outward observation. Nor is it a supplement to positive action and acquisition. Rather, imagination can serve the artist best as a "buffer zone" between system and dogma, positive action and the immense possibility of negation, which is the source of all creative ideas (Gould, 1984c).

Gould (1968d) denoted in his writings that inspiration is a form of knowing. Gould thought that the inspired artist employs both intellect and inspiration in the creative process. He upheld that the two parts of the creative artist's psyche—namely, intellect and inspiration—were balanced in the highly effective artist. He disagreed with Nadia Boulanger's claim that the genius artist was an artist with only inspiration. Gould (1984b) mentioned that the function of intellectual speculation is also involved in the creative process. But he warned that too much speculation might paralyze the creative process. He wrote that there are personal limits to speculation.

We can also know music through the ear's capacity to discriminate. Gould advanced the idea that the ear has the following capabilities: (1) It can discriminate multiple voices, same or various colors; (2) More than three simultaneous notes can be heard; (3) It can hear alterations in pitch, quarter tones, and tempered tuning; (4) It can hear multiple sources of sound (e.g., four corners of a room) (Gould, 1969e). These abilities are especially useful in knowing music with contrapuntal textures.

WHAT IS THE RELATIONSHIP OF THE PERFORMER TO MUSICAL KNOWLEDGE?

The performer's knowledge of music should be based on mental imagery. Ideally, the performer knows music through the mind first, and then through the physical reality. The physical manifestations of music were secondary to Gould. He stressed the mental and spiritual sides of music. For example, he wrote of piano technique as mental imagery,

> . . . one does not play the piano with one's fingers, one plays the piano with one's mind. . . . If you have a clear image of what you want to do there's no reason it should ever need reinforcement. If you don't, all the fine Czerny studies and Hanon exercises in the world aren't going to help. (Dubal, 1984, p. 183).

The performer's knowledge is from within and can complement the composer's view. "The performer has to have faith that he is doing, even blindly, the right thing, that he may be finding interpretive possibilities not wholly realized even by the composer." What is the nature of this knowledge? Gould believed the performer knows from inner revelations (Gould, undated, media transcript, "Glenn Gould interviewed by Bernard Asbell").

Gould took a liberal view concerning the performer's tactile knowledge of a composition. He maintained that fingering should be a spontaneous knowledge, except in rare instances when the music is written against the grain of the keyboard. He claimed that no amount of academic systematization could help. Solutions to fingering problems should be worked out for each situation as it presents itself. Of his own playing, he wrote, "I've never played anything the same way three times and I can't even conceive of anybody doing that" (Gould, 1980b, p. 11).

Gould (1980b) could not understand practicing in order to achieve a connection with the keyboard. He thought more of practicing as a means to determine relationships and structural balances within the music. Gould held that practicing should be idea-centered and not mechanical.

What Is the Relationship of Knowing and Musical Pedagogy?

Gould (1984) wrote that composers and performers are spared the temptation of manufacturing ready-made answers to artistic problems. Musicians involved in pedagogy are not so lucky. The teacher's role is a dangerous and difficult one. Very often teachers are prone to oversimplification, and thus, distortion for the sake of providing quick answers. It is also a great temptation for the teacher to try to verbalize every situation in order to have an answer for the student.

Gould (1980b) was opposed to oververbalizing in especially tactile matters. He insisted that one must be unconscious of the tactile processes when performing. If one verbalized this then the spontaneous knowledge would be lost. Gould wrote that when one verbalizes the processes that make things work for you, "there is always the danger that you will become conscious of exactly what it is that you're doing and then your mental relationship with that process becomes a factor that will inhibit the spontaneity" (Gould, 1980b, p. 9).

On learning to play an instrument, Gould (1980b) was concerned that the mechanistic aspect not be stressed too much. He considered it to be relatively unimportant compared to the far more important matter of inner awareness in making music meaningful.

Gould believed that practicing slavishly at an instrument was unnecessary. He wrote, ". . . when you're translating music onto the instrument, there should be an immediate connection when you look at it, a connection which, if you have it, renders that kind of practice completely unnecessary." He could not understand the complaint of many pianists that they were stiff from not being at the keyboard. Gould argued that performance is more mental than athletic (Gould, 1980b, pp. 10–11).

Often, when Gould practiced, he would create a filter of ambient noise so that he could not physically hear the sounds of his playing. Rather, he could concentrate on the tactile impressions he was making and inner imagination. He held that this was the way in which children should be encouraged to play a musical instrument. Their inner imaginations would be the source of their knowledge, not the physical manifestations. This methodology would also promote musical concentration (Gould, from fragments of a draft of Prospects of Recording, Glenn Gould Collection).

Gould was once asked the question, can students be taught individuality in their performances? Gould responded by offering the following suggestions for increasing individuality:

1) Students should stop listening to each other before they have determined their own concept of the music. After they have established an individual

relationship with the music then they can listen to their colleagues;

2) They should not formulate their musical concept based on some alleged interpretive system. Artists should not have any academically imposed parameters for their art other than those that emanate from music history;

3) The teacher might record the student, play back the performance, and then pose questions that would lead the student to greater understanding (e.g., Are you satisfied with this performance?);

4) The teacher should pose several lead questions in the instructional process (e.g., Are you satisfied with the entire delivery, the sense of pace, etc.? What areas need to change pace to give more tense or relaxed atmosphere?). Gould (1980b) understood "pace" not to mean the actual tempo but a sense of involvement, of "structural motivation."

Gould (1978a) maintained that musicians' hearing very often limits their understanding and imagination because they bring preconceptions to the listening experience. They possess their personal tactile presumptions of what is possible and that attitude often limits their vision of what is possible.

Finally, Gould (1984b) wrote that it is a problem when musicians forget the artificiality of the musical systems in which they work. Those who are entrenched in their musical systems lose the replenishment of invention, the basis for creative ideas. It is also a knowledge that one must be open to negation that is outside one's known musical system in order to be creative.

IDEAS FOR A MORALITY OF MUSIC

DOES MUSIC POSSESS MORAL IMPLICATIONS?

Gould (1974b) indicated that he agreed with the Platonic contention that music influences morality. He maintained that music possesses moral implications in that an aesthetic decision could influence a moral judgment and musical integrity inherently possesses a kind of moral imperative.

AESTHETIC DECISIONS AND MORAL JUDGMENT

Gould (1974b) wrote that if one were able to persuade a person that a particular aesthetic practice represented a moral implication, then one was responsible to do so. Society, as a whole, can improve only if the individual members, including the musical artist, are conscious of their social responsibility and modify their private attitudes. Gould (1978e) advanced the notion that it is the moral responsibility of the artist to engage in artistic activity that would be aimed at the betterment of humanity.

The notion that one can successfully separate word and deed is linked to the occidental tradition of attachment to freedom of movement and speech. In this regard, Gould (1984b) didn't find any problem in reconciling the individual conscience aspect of the Reformation and the collective censorship of the puritan tradition. Since he believed that the puritan tradition involved perpetual schismatic division, it was considered as a forward-looking phenomenon. He prided himself to be the "last puritan."

In a similar light, Gould (1972) declared that the banalities of middle-class America have impeded its moral and cultural evolution. The freedoms of America have not necessarily promoted moral and cultural growth. Gould thought that to be locked into cultural affectations is to be in moral bondage. Gould advocated that people develop a sensitive regard for moral issues even if it meant abandoning comfortable life-styles.

Gould asserted that he preferred to suspend aesthetic opinions and make only moral judgments when assessing the work of others. He wrote, "I do try as best I can to make only moral judgments and not aesthetic ones—except . . . in the case of my own work" (Gould, 1974b, p. 75). Gould (1984b) imagined the aesthetic touches on moral values as well as theological. Gould espoused aesthetic values that included moral overtones like a lack of ostentation, a lack of exhibitionism, and a rejection of fake virtuosity. In their place he advocated serenity, nostalgia, and classical purity.

MUSICAL INTEGRITY AS A MORAL IMPERATIVE

Musical integrity represented a kind of moral standard in Gould's mind. For the musically honest artist there is no room for compromise. Artistic judgments must be grounded in truth and personal inspiration. If one must make an artistic decision, one must make the valid choice even if it means inconvenience and difficulty.

Gould (1965f) highly criticized all who compromised in art, including institutions like the CBC. He disapproved of the CBC's corporate, middle-of-the-road choices in presenting musical works. He was incensed that decisions were made on the basis of extramusical matters. He also thought that quality programming could be achieved under the right artistic leadership.

LIVE ARTS AS IMMORAL ACTIVITY AND POTENTIALLY MENACING

Gould (1981) found the live arts to be immoral. He argued that voyeuristically watching a human being in a nonpragmatic testing situation was cruel, pointless, and ultimately wrong. It is morally wrong for one to derive pleasure from the struggles, weaknesses, or mishaps of others in performing situations. He wrote, "I have always had grave misgivings about the motives of people who go to concerts, live theatre, whatever" (Gould, 1981, p. 18)

In this context, he also had misgivings about the role of the critic as commentator in performance situations. Because the critic usually focuses on aesthetic values rather than moral ones, Gould (1974b) found the critic to be a morally endangered species.

Gould (1974b) thought art to be a menace in that it has the potential to influence moral behavior. He was recon-

ciled with the notion that art should be monitored, like in
the Soviet Union, for the moral good of the community.

Technology and Morality in Art

Gould (1974b) did not view technology as a compromising,
dehumanizing intrusion into art. Rather, Gould (1981)
advocated that technology has the ability to morally
redeem the artist. He wrote, "Technology had positioned
itself between the attempt and the realization; the 'charity
of the machine,' to quote the theologian Jean LeMoyne,
had interposed itself between the frailty of nature and the
vision of the idealized accomplishment" (Gould, 1984b, p.
345).

Gould (1980b) admired the work of Jean LeMoyne,
especially in a concept taken from the theology of Teilhard
de Chardin: the Christification of the machine. The most
practical and apparently mechanical operations of machin-
ery possess a more profound level. Gould considered this
idea very profound and meaningful in his life.

Gould held an almost mystical belief in technology's
power to mediate human activity. He wrote, "Technology
introduces a protective shield around humanity which
removes the necessity for humans to measure themselves
against one another, on either a bodily or a psychical scale"
(Gould, 1984b, p. 445).

Technology redeems the artist by replacing the awful,
degrading, humanly damaging uncertainties of the live
concert experience. Gould advocated the development of
the artist as an emotionally and spiritually integrated
person. The live concert experience often leaves artists
psychologically wounded and helps them to develop
behaviors that are spiritually and morally untrue to their
real identities. Very often negative behaviors develop that
pull artists away from their personal centers.

Technology redeems the artist by taking the specific
personal performance information out of the musical
experience. That information could potentially detract
from the essence of the musical experience and the

creation of a contemplative climate. Gould wrote, "Whether the performer is going to climb the musical Everest on this particular occasion no longer matters. And it's for that reason that the word 'immoral' comes into the picture" (Gould, 1981, p. 18). Gould believed that if we as a culture ignore technology's capability of redemption, then that is immoral because we are ignoring a great boon for culture.

Technology possesses a unique capacity for dissection, analysis, and idealization. It embodies a dimension that carries us to look inward in depth and begin a life of meditation and contemplation. Gould agreed with Marshall McLuhan's statement,

> What we fail to notice, however, is the profoundly oriental effect of electronic technology on ourselves, as we look inward in depth and begin this inscrutable life of inner meditation and the contemplation with electronic circuitry—it carries us inward all the time. (Gould, 1965c)

Recording technology, in particular, can redeem the artist by helping to perfect a structure through creative deception. There is no area more occupied with philosophical debates than the aims and techniques of recording (Gould, 1984b). Gould declared that recordings that are made in a sort of snapshot context "immunizes the music at hand against the benefactions of technology" (Gould, 1984b, p. 358). In order to answer the criticism that communication between artist and listener occurs best in the live concert hall, Gould wrote there are those who claim that the truest communication occurs between artist and audience in live performance. It is there that the high drama of human communion can take place. Gould counters by stating that art on its most noble mission is hardly human at all (Gould, 1962e).

Gould professed that there is an essential humanity in this use of technology. Technology in art becomes a higher calling. Gould wrote, ". . . through its mediation one could transcend the frailty of nature and concentrate on a vision of the ideal" (Gould, 1983a, p. 183). Through technology, we have the ability to remove ourselves from ourselves and achieve a state of ecstasy.

Technology enables the artist to potentially promote musical integrity by creating a climate of anonymity; by allowing the artist the time and freedom to prepare a thoughtful conception of the musical work; and by allowing the musical artist to perfect a statement without having to worry about trivia like nerves, finger slips, etc.

Technology imposes upon art an idea of morality which transcends that notion of art itself (Gould, 1974b). Because Gould considered art to be potentially destructive, he favored the thought that art should be given the chance to phase itself out. He wrote, ". . . once introduced into the circuitry of art, the technological presence must be encoded and decoded—in such a way that its presence is, in every respect, at the service of that spiritual good that ultimately will serve to banish art itself" (Gould, 1984b, pp. 446–447). Gould envisioned a higher moral good that transcends art. He wrote further,

> I feel that art should be given the chance to phase itself out. I think that we must accept the fact that art is not inevitably benign, that it is potentially destructive. We should analyze the areas where it tends to do least harm, use them as a guideline, and build into art a component that will enable it to preside over its own obsolescence. (Gould, 1974b, p. 77)

CAN THE MUSICIAN FRAME PERSONAL VALUES FOR A MORAL ARTISTRY?

Gould (1984, 1980d) professed that the musician not only could, but should frame positive values for a moral artistry. It is through these values that one should attempt a transformation of the spirit, in the light of which one must try to live out one's life. Gould advocated a value construct that would promote the philosophical measure of the musician-artist. By philosophical measure Gould meant how the musician stands before the presence of a moral and artistic antithesis. Philosophical measure gives the musician perspective and dimension in the midst of negation.

Negation reduces everything in our life of concepts and ideas. Consequently, the uncertainty and fragility of our systems are exposed without our artificial barricades and logics against negation. Negation potentially stimulates our invention like no other concept.

Gould described the phenomenon of moral challenge that each artist potentially faces when he quoted Nietzsche's words, "Man is a rope stretched between the animal and the superman—the rope over an abyss." Gould professed that it was "the precarious traversal of that rope that stimulated the creative juices of artists like Schoenberg. To such men, isolation fashioned a hero's life and heroism was the patron of creativity" (Gould, 1973d). The reckoning of spiritual transformation grapples with these uncertainties.

WHAT ARE SOME VALUES FOR FRAMING A MORALITY FOR MUSICIANS?

Gould (1976e, 1964d) said that extramusical perspectives were the only means he had of trying to discover a moral basis for his discussions concerning morality in art. Thus, a morality of music is concerned with music's dynamic within the context of several human dimensions. This does not mean that moral values for musicians should be legislated or written into the social framework. Rather, music must remain disengaged from the constraints that govern the community. Music should be monitored within a separate framework of values that include a moral consciousness.

A lack of spiritual substance in a musical work distressed Gould (1976d) since he continually sought depth in his art. Gould vigorously advocated the following values for the musician to act with moral artistry.

- The musician should dispense with the "yoke of respectability." If the artistic norms that are considered respectable interfere with the musician's artistic vision, then these conditionals should be avoided. In his own life Gould defied the conservatory system that put a premium on expressivity, languor in performance. He preferred to turn the expressive conventions of his day on their head (Cott, 1984). He rejected the artificial symbols of status, competitiveness, etc., promulgated by society as false and misleading. Gould (1967d) judged that they lead away from rather than to the truth.

- Musicians should recognize the fact that it is a moral-aesthetic problem to artificially attempt to evaluate artistic achievements only by a process of "historical summation of collective chronology." Anonymity is a way in which the artist can cancel the competitive intimidation of chronology (Gould, 1973c). Artists must have the total freedom to work outside chronological perspectives. And indeed, there have been several creative musical minds (e.g., Richard Strauss) who have defied the process of historical evolution (Gould, 1962a).

- It is desirable for composers to employ conscience in their musical decisions. Although Gould did not offer an in-depth explanation of the meaning of conscience, he did imply in his writings that it was a superior activity for a composer to involve conscience in the compositional process. He also outlined qualities desirable for the formation of conscience.

    Gould used Schoenberg's music as an example of a composer employing conscience in the creative process. He wrote, ". . . on a purely technical level it reveals something of the spiritual metamorphosis which sought stability amidst the attraction of conflicting poles of influence at every level of emotional experience, and, above all, it reveals an impeccable conscience involved in a perpetual search which became its dedication" (Gould, 1953b, p. 23).

- The musician should work with sensitivity towards the fact that every artistic decision can be equated with a moral correlative. Therefore, it is desirable for the musician to avoid negative, corrupt behavior. Gould

(1975a) categorized aggression in art to be an example of such undesirable behavior. Aggression focuses the attention of the artist on worldly successes rather than artistic perfection. A nonaggressive attitude would help to promote art as a humanly transcendent experience which is a superior, spiritual good.

Closely related to aggression is the "art-as-violence surrogate" theory. Gould argued that this position avoided the real issue of humanity's spiritual growth. He wrote, "I don't believe in surrogates; they're simply the playthings of minds resistant to the perfectability of man. Besides, if you are looking for violent surrogates, genetic engineering is a better bet" (Gould, 1974b, p. 76).

- Music should not be reduced to a level of self-serving activity (Gould, 1976). This distressed Gould since he believed that a lack of spiritual substance in a musical work resulted from a self-serving attitude. He continually sought ways that promoted inner depth in art. One way was his campaign against applause. The fact that applause promotes self-serving activity caused Gould to reject applause. He asserted that applause should be eliminated in order to free the artist from distraction. Applause was considered by Gould to be an external, shallow, public manifestation that detracted from the real purpose and value of art.

Gould (1962e) wrote of the purpose of art as a life-long pursuit of wonder and serenity. Art is not just a momentary experience, but should awaken each person to contemplatively create their own divinity. Gould praised the work of artists who achieved contemplative repose in their work (e.g., Rosalind Tureck's performance of Bach). Gould wrote, "It was playing of such uprightness, to put it into the moral sphere. There was such a sense of a repose that had nothing to do with languor, but rather with moral rectitude in the liturgical sense" (Gould, 1957). This state of introspection has been especially facilitated by radio and recording. Through these media the listener is better able to focus on the music and not any self-centered affectations of a performer (Gould, 1962e).

Gould (1977b, 1962e, 1981) claimed that composers like Ockeghem and Gesualdo represent the ideal, contemplative state articulated best in their creative work. Gould felt a spiritual attachment to Gibbon's music for the same reason. And, Gould wrote, "Sibelius was disinclined to provide for virtuoso display." Composers like Liszt, Chopin, and Schubert represent the more flamboyant, superficial approach to music. These composers' works are filled with "empty theatrical gestures" that are full of exhibitionism and worldly hedonistic qualities.

Musicians can employ a sensual quality in their music while avoiding extrovert theatrics. Gould (1953) advocated drama in music but considered the theatrical in both composition and performance as limiting and immoral. Music that possessed drama without theatrical overtones was most desirable. Consequently, he objected to any music that he judged exhibitionistic.

CONCERTO

Gould proposed that the concerto form is an example of a musical structure that features theatrical overtones. In describing the conventions of the concerto structure, Gould wrote,

> the orchestral pre-exposition setup, to titillate the listener's expectation of a grand dramatic entrance for the soloist; the tiresomely repetitive thematic structure, arranged to let the soloist prove that he really can turn that phrase to a more rakish tilt than the fellow on first clarinet who just announced it; and above all the outdated aristocracy of cadenza writing—the posturing trills and arpeggios, all twitteringly superfluous to the fundamental thematic proposition. All these have helped to build a concerto tradition which has provided some of the most embarrassing musical examples of the primeval human need for

showing off. All these have helped to substantiate the outrageous ego of the soloist. (Gould, 1984b, pp. 70–71).

Gould (1962g) reflected on the commonly accepted notion of his day when he said that the concerto form appears to be an unserviceable vehicle for modern compositional techniques. Gould speculated that future composers will find other forms, "other means to satisfy the primeval human need for showing off."

Gould attempted to integrate the elements of the concerto in his performances. He wrote of his performance of the Brahms d-minor concerto that one could either perform the work in the fashionable, romantic way, stressing drama, contrasts, inequalities, masculine versus feminine contrasts, etc.; or one could envision the future in Brahms as a sophisticated interweaving of a fundamental motivic strand, one can read into it the analytical standpoints of our own day.

Another example of what Gould called theatrical music was Mozart's mature period music. Gould lost interest in Mozart's music for the following reasons. Mozart employed theatrical gestures in his operas and instrumental music. This exemplified the "hedonism of the eighteenth century theater" (Cott, 1984, p. 56). Gould considered Mozart's music to be very repetitive. Gould described it as "cut from the same cookie stamp. I think that as Mozart became relatively successful as a theatrical craftsman, his instrumental compositions declined in interest very rapidly" (Cott, 1984, p. 57).

Gould claimed that he recorded Mozart because he disapproved of Mozart's worldly way. Gould wrote,

> my ambition for that project was that it would rid those pieces of their frivolous, theatrical accoutrements. I wanted to bypass such diversions with the help of firm, baroquish tempos, and to create, from the rather promising material of alberti basses, the suggestion of secondary voices and, hence, the illusion of a contrapuntal aspect—of a life of the spirit—of which Mozart, in my view, is essentially innocent. (Gould, 1978f, p. 45)

Gould said in a phone conversation with Oliver Daniel that "as long as Mozart doesn't as yet have his own theatrical identity . . . I like him . . . the moment he gets it, I don't like him" (Gould, 1978h, transcript of a telephone conversation with Oliver Daniel, p. 6).

Gould (1964b, 1969c) considered it immoral to show off in performance. He insisted that extramusical considerations should be subordinated to the organic processes of the music. Consequently, Gould was opposed to the revival of rare romantics since he considered it a manifestation of a kind of virtuoso-cult revival.

THE MISSION OF MORALITY

The transformation of the spirit was central to Gould's morality. One way this is achieved is for the artist to become a philosopher. In Gould's autobiographical media project called the "Solitude Trilogy," metaphors are presented pointing to the direction the artist must take in order to become a philosopher.

In the "Idea of North" the artist is told to go north, to go upward in the direction of individual decisions that transform the spirit. Going north is a purification process that is personal and singular for the artist (Gould, 1984b). The "Idea of North" is a metaphor for the artist's struggle against human nature and its limitations. North is a metaphor for the war against Mother Nature. The moral equivalent for us is to go north. North helps us to view life on a different scale. One does not achieve north easily. It is the product of inner conflict of values, a dialectic that emerges when one pursues the ideals of north (Gould, 1967–1968). North is also a metaphor for isolation and living a puritan life (Gould, 1974b).

"The Latecomers" is a metaphor for the cost of nonconformity. Newfoundland is an isolated province caught between two cultures, its spiritual origins and its economic ties to greater Canada. Gould (1969d) describes its people as being removed from the center of society. But because they are removed they can see it more clearly. They have a way of life that is in the mainstream but not of it.

"Quiet in the Land" also emphasizes existential separateness. Gould has one of the characters say, "I think we need to learn, really to get on in this world of ours without becoming tainted by it. And that's really what great art is all about, isn't it? I mean, that's what a fugue, ultimately, is all about—using, if you will, the techniques that the composer had at his disposal and making something of it which is really quite other worldly" (Gould, 1975g, p. 5). This radio documentary also talks about the artist leading a simple life, concentrating on a few things and doing them well. This life-view is a kind of faith and faith can be expressed in many different ways. We are strangers here; we are pilgrims here.

Another mission of morality is the creation of disengagement from biological limitation. Gould believed that recordings are "one of the best metaphors we have for it" (Gould, 1984b, p. 355). He also wrote that "we very often tend to confuse a sense of humanity with the way in which human concerns are traditionally resolved" (Gould, 1984b, p. 356). Many people think that humanity unaided is humanity's best advocate. Gould argued that this is the most unwarranted, antihuman assumption of the post-Renaissance period.

The highest mission of a superior morality is to remove ourselves from ourselves and achieve a state of ecstasy (Gould, 1983a). Gould wrote, ". . . the ultimate achievement for 'creative opter-outers' is the cultivation of a state of ecstasy" (Gould, 1978b, p. 16). He thought that "ecstasy is a commodity most frequently purveyed by fugal situations" (Gould, 1973b).

CONTRAPUNTAL TEXTURES AND MORALITY

For Gould (1962e), contrapuntal textures were a metaphor representing a moral life of the spirit. Contrapuntal textures iconically represented those qualities of life that

Gould considered most desirable and moral. At the core of this thought is the notion that the voices in contrapuntal textures are perceived as equal. This iconically symbolizes nonegoist, nonaggressive, nontheatrical behavior that promotes a life of the spirit. In addition, the voices typify a gesture that expresses the anonymity dynamic. Within the milieu of anonymity one can place spiritual focus on the transcendent. Any narcissistic preoccupation is replaced by a transcendent conscience.

The energy in contrapuntal textures feels endless and points to the infinite. It can generate a contemplative sense of repose. The concept of repose is not a lack of energy, but rather, the product of an internal metamorphosis. It is an amalgam of ecstasy and reason. Gould considered qualities of sublime resignation as the ultimate achievements of great age and wisdom. He wrote of "that transfiguring light of ultimate philosophic repose" (Gould, 1962a, p. 49).

6. CONCLUSIONS FOR A PHILOSOPHY OF MUSIC

INTRODUCTION

Philosophical inquiry stresses broad generalizations and results in inclusive meanings. One can learn to know the meaning of complex sets of variables by using the philosophical method. The conclusions presented here are the result of such inquiry. The author's purpose was to synthesize, integrate, and arrive at an interpretation of Glenn Gould's philosophical thought about music.

At first glance, Gould's thought appears to be an impenetrable tangle of disparate ideas. Upon deeper investigation, one can discover a pattern of thought, unusually consistent and all-embracing, that emerges from the seemingly chaotic grid.

It was clearly established earlier that Gould offered ideas for the formation of a philosophical construct of music. Questions arise out of the speculation about these ideas. Which, if any, of these notions does Gould favor in his contribution to the philosophy of music? Each leading theory of music and music education stresses a different method in dealing with its problems or issues. Consequently, each theory highlights a disparate set of values. Where does Gould's thought stand in relation to these conflicting approaches?

This chapter is devoted to a discussion about the Gouldian model for a philosophy of music and its relationship with the leading theories of music. It should be noted here that the Gouldian model is not only a paradigm for a philosophy of music but an autobiography of Gould's spiritual life.

The ideas presented must not be considered the final word about Gould. Gould's thought is so rich it suggests many different kinds and levels of interpretation. This book is but one perspective that will hopefully lead to future lines of fruitful, challenging research.

THE GOULDIAN MODEL FOR A PHILOSOPHY OF MUSIC

It appears that much of Gould's intellectual output can be integrated into three primary levels of thought: a morality of music, a sociology of music, and an epistemology of music.

A MORALITY OF MUSIC

When one is faced with Gould's thought one senses that it presents a dynamic set of values rooted in his personal vision. Indeed, his moral understanding radiates from inner awareness and not from worn-out dogmas. At the apex of the Gouldian model are ideas for a morality of music. All other ideas appear to be dominated by and subordinated to Gould's moral consciousness.

Gould stands unique in the company of other modern thinkers of music. He courageously tangled with musical issues in the light of their moral implications. He not only speculated about music and morality but lived a key moral premise of his philosophical thought: the artist drew insight from inner, personal knowledge rather than from outside influences.

It seems Gould was disillusioned with existing musical conventions and sought redemption from them. He devised a theology for himself and others that took on the seriousness of a religion. His creed adopted an anticonvention for convention's sake stance that called him forth to find personal transcendence in order to achieve the redemption implied by freedom. It challenged him to liberate himself from factors that limit spiritual development.

As a consequence, Gould challenged all artists to rethink not only the answers but the *questions* of how music relates to the world. He poses interesting moral insights concerning music's importance to humanity and the musician's importance to culture.

OVERVIEW OF THE RELATIONSHIP OF MUSIC TO MORALITY

Before one examines the uncommon (or unusual) position Glenn Gould held concerning music and morality it is expedient to review how this problematic relationship has been presented by others.

There are those who would deny any relationship of music to morality on the grounds that music means nothing outside of its congeneric dimensions. (The term "congeneric" was coined by Wilson Coker (1972) to mean the intrinsic dynamics of a music.) Historically, the view that music means nothing outside its internal syntax can be traced as far back as Empiricus of the Third Century (Epperson, 1967).

The formalist rationale evolved as a result of that position. Formalists deny music's power to express anything extramusical. Their approach was advocated by Hanslick and Gurney in the nineteenth century, and by Stravinsky and Hindemith, among others, in the twentieth century.

Leonard B. Meyer (1956) held a somewhat more modified posture. He developed a theory of the relationship of musical stimuli to emotional responses, confirming that music gives rise to emotions. Susanne K. Langer (1942) differed from Meyer's viewpoint in that she proposed that emotions represented and conveyed by music were not actual emotions but emotional forms or virtual emotions that resemble real emotions. Swanger (1985) maintained that because music embodies the principle of ambivalence it does not possess a single meaning, and therefore, cannot provide moral insight.

We can trace the opposing view that music might embody moral implications from the fifth century B.C. to the present. The Pythagoreans held that music possesses ethical value that should be used in the attainment of sound morality. They envisioned music, by virtue of its numerical basis, as a force for moral good (Epperson, 1967).

Plato maintained in his *Laws* and *Republic* that music can move the emotions, thereby instructing the soul and influencing one's moral behavior. Plato argued that music, as an educational discipline, should be utilized to promote the good life (Portnoy, 1954). The ancient Greeks imagined that music educates one to feel pleasure and pain properly, and thus, disposes a person towards moral goodness (Schoen, 1972). Portnoy explained this belief in writing, "Music thereby took on a teleological function which should help in the attainment of a sound morality" (Portnoy, 1954, p. 21).

Since the Greeks believed that simplicity best reflects the moral order of the universe, it was thought that the most ideal music to achieve this end was direct, simple music. Musical simplicity was judged to be reflective of the temperance of the soul (Epperson, 1967).

Aristotle concurred with the Platonic vision that music instructs, disposes one towards moral virtue, and has the power to mold character (Epperson, 1967). He said that although music does not touch reason directly it nonetheless orients one towards virtue (Schoen, 1972). In the history of Western aesthetics there are others (like Tolstoy, Schiller, John Gardner, and Busoni) who have theorized that music possesses moral character because it has the power to instruct.

Callen stated that music can be an opportunity for reflection on the presence or absence of dispositions, sympathetic, empathetic, or emulative, in everyday life by comparison with the sorts of expressive traits one is able to respond to in music (Callen, 1982).

Finally, Callen provided another insight into how music can lead to moral import. His theory revolves around the claim that music is expressively dynamic (i.e., because its expressive character is constantly changing, the features of a composition go through a metamorphosis of stress and relaxation).

This phenomenon, in a sense, mirrors the emotional flux in one's life. Through a sympathetic response generated by imaginative identification, music becomes morally significant because it "can give us a better sense of the range and refinement of our own sensibility" (Callen, 1982, p. 390).

THE GOULDIAN MORAL IMPERATIVE

How does Gould's thought about morality and music relate to the ideas presented above? Clearly, Gould's thought is sympathetic to the Platonic notion that music possesses the power to affect our moral decisions. Gould believed that music is endowed with moral implications in that an aesthetic decision could influence a moral judgment, and musical integrity inherently possesses a kind of moral imperative (Gould, 1974b; 1978).

The Gouldian moral imperative frames moral approaches for music. Three such approaches are found earlier in this book: advocation of musical integrity, the recognition that the live arts may be immoral activity, and the use of technology as a boon for a moral life in music.

In his advocation of musical integrity, Gould kept the high standards normally advocated for musical practice in the world of classical music. However, he ventured beyond common applications of musical integrity (e.g., faithfulness to the score, working for technical mastery) in order to frame broader parameters of artistic practice. These call for personal, as well as artistic, honesty.

Gould intuitively sensed, as did Kupperman (1978), that the boundaries of morality are fluid. Thus, he imagined for the present and future world an existential model that would expand the awareness of musical integrity in music makers. The kind of moral uprightness he called for was an honesty with oneself, in interactions with the world, and finally, with the music (that should be a product of personal conscientiousness).

There is no room for compromising musical integrity in the works of Gould (1965f). He, like Plato and Marxists, considered music's power as a potential societal force. He warned that the live arts are potentially dangerous because live performance affects our moral awareness, and often, promotes types of behavior that are wrong. For example, he was opposed to the voyeuristic potentiality in the live musical performance (Gould, 1981). He called critics a morally endangered species because they ignored what Gould felt were the important meanings and issues of performance, namely, the moral, spiritual implications (Gould, 1974b).

Gould's ideas about performance are very similar to Aristotle's in his *Politics,* Bk VII, Chapter V, 1341b:

> . . . the performer practices the art, not for the sake of his own improvement but in order to give pleasure, and that of a vulgar sort to his hearers. For this reason the execution of such music is not the part of a freeman but of a paid performer, and the result is that the performers are vulgarized for the end at which they aim is bad. The vulgarity of the spectator tends to lower the character of the music and therefore of the performers; they look to him—he makes them what they are, and fashions even their bodies by the movements which he expects them to exhibit. (Portnoy, 1954, p. 27)

Gould raised the consciousness of the performer to be aware that performance can alienate one from one's spiritual center. The audience can possibly assume an ugly countenance in that the performer is dehumanized, objectified, set apart, torn apart, fragmented by the psychological dynamic between the audience and the performer. Gould suggested that music is an intimate activity, like love making, that should not be impersonalized and distracted by the audience/performer relationship.

He warned that the spiritual meanings of music are destroyed or circumvented in performance by baser interworkings that rob the artist and the audience of a true connection with the music. However, Gould offered hope in that the evolution of the audience/performer relationship does not necessarily have to end with prevalent practice. The liabilities of performance can be removed by the intervention of technology.

Technology redeems music from the dehumanizing aspects of live performance by replacing humanly damaging uncertainties of live concerts, allowing the artist greater freedom to be psychologically centered, helping to rid performances of the focus on gestures and other manifestations that detract from the essence of the music, and offering greater potentiality for analysis, dissection, and thus, greater musical understanding. Through technology the artist is better able to transcend the imperfect natural order and possibly achieve moral goodness.

Gould (1984b) recognized the profound levels of meaning technology could offer humanity. It not only could mediate human activity but impose upon art an idea of morality that transcends the notion of art itself. In the Gouldian universe, art will be at the service of spiritual good. Art will ideally stand for its true purpose: the facilitation of the moral good in a future social order.

Gould saw technology's potential to transcend the limitations of the so-called natural world. He intuitively understood technology's potential, in Heideggerian terms, to reveal, to challenge forth freedom. This is a special freedom that is not caused by the human will but, in Heidegger's words, "governs the open in the sense of the cleared and lighted up, i.e. of the revealed. It is the happening of revealing, i.e. of truth" (Heidegger, 1977, p. 25).

Because technology possesses the potential to open us up to experience the freedom of openness, Gould (1981) wrote that it would be immoral to ignore technology's power to redeem our lives. We are morally reduced if we do not use technology for the moral good.

It is this Gouldian moral imperative that redefines the commonly accepted relationship of music to morality. Music is stretched towards a morality of creative openness and goodness that is transnatural and responsible to all living and nonliving things. The moral, musical, and philosophical ranges are immeasurably enriched through the exploration of this notion.

It is impossible to separate Gould the artist from Gould the moralist. His moral and musical visions are remarkably and inextricably intertwined. Literally hundreds of written statements and media projects confirm Gould's passion to frame a morality for music that endows music and music makers with singular spiritual significance. Gould's moral imperative allays life-thwarting anxiety by conferring profound importance to music and musicians. This stance promotes a psychological wellness and wholeness for the musician, who is encouraged to cultivate what Paul Tillich calls "the courage to be" (Tillich, 1952).

THE GOULDIAN MORALITY OF CREATIVE OPENNESS

Gould recognized the spiritual importance of being creatively in touch with one's inner self (Gould, 1964b). It is only when one knows oneself that greater spiritual depth occurs and one can reach out to others in social and moral justice. Artistic expression, practiced within the sphere of a morality of creative openness, is a way for one to better understand the self and others. Gould proposed that music uniquely lends itself to this kind of personal revelation (Gould, 1980b).

Gould organized his life down to the minutest detail in order to participate in an intimate relationship with his inner voice. By finely tuning and focusing his life's energy on selected projects, he heightened his self-knowledge. Something of value and elegance emerged from his open understanding of the inner life.

Gould knew that when one cuts off the listening to one's inner voice a crisis of the human spirit develops. Subsequently, our interpersonal relationships are retarded and suffer. Robbins writes of this phenomenon, ". . . failure to risk being what is growing in me is the failure of the whole human race" (Robbins, 1985, p. 12).

Robbins further stated that "As we discover what blocks us from expressing our most creative selves, remove these blocks, and allow ourselves to be the artists we truly are, we recreate the world and old injustices fall away" (Robbins, 1985, p. 13). Creative activity can no longer be left to only the so-called artists. Creativity must find its way into everyone's daily activities.

We must make a quantum leap with Gould and establish a reciprocal relationship between ourselves and the Gouldian formulations of creative openness if we are to begin to understand Gould. He is not easily understood since he often ventures beyond ethical reasoning to an aesthetic meaning of morality that goes deeper than reasoned ethics. We must, in a phenomenological sense, "presence ourselves" to the implied, subtle moral range that Gould offered.

Gould's extraordinary moral sensitivity stretches out beyond the usual moral themes and parameters as outlined by moralists like Kupperman (1978). Kupperman wrote that we are much more likely to consider behavior moral if it involves serious harm to an individual or society (Kupperman, 1977). Gould's moral limits appear to be more finely tuned than Kupperman's approach since Gould embraces the whole of a person's spirituality.

Gould's moral sensibility is similar to Gabriel Moran's notion of a transnatural morality of goodness, which speaks of the interdependence of all life and our responsibility to all living and nonliving forms. The transnatural morality of goodness points to a goodness that emanates from the welling-up and overflowing of being. It is creativity grounded in endless being (Moran, 1987).

It is a creative moral sense that includes even technology, for although it is respectful of nature, it is not limited by nature. Under this rubric one realizes that creativity comes from the most sacred part of ourselves, the part that yields to creative openness. Gould instinctively followed this path by employing artistic techniques and methods that transcended what was commonly thought of as the natural, moral way to do things (e.g., recording techniques, radio documentaries).

Gouldian artistic gestures are creatively moral and suggest a comprehensive reverence in everyday activities that informs our person. We can look to Robbins for a better understanding of this kind of reverence. She wrote, ". . . reverence, is seeing compassionately, allowing the 'object' simply to be what it is. Every sense can become sacramental in this experience; even ordinary food becomes eucharistic" (Robbins, 1985, p. 98). This is creativity-centered morality that sees creativity as moral activity because it has the power to affect our spirituality.

GOULD AND MORAL IMAGERY

Gould employed language rich in imagery in order to communicate his creation-centered moral philosophy of music. Contrapuntal imagery, in particular, is significant in much of his work. This is evident in his performance style, as well as the uncommon creative techniques used in recordings, compositions, and other media projects. Gould used contrapuntal imagery as a metaphor for a life-plan rooted in spiritual (moral) principles.

CONTRAPUNTAL IMAGERY

A moral life of the spirit is portrayed in contrapuntal imagery (Gould, 1962e). Contrapuntal textures iconically represent those qualities of life that Gould considered most desirable and moral (i.e., selflessness, the capacity to know the self as part of the interrelated world, and the ability to tolerate ambiguity or the unknown).

The voices in contrapuntal textures are often perceived as equally weighted in importance. This can signify nonegoistic, nonaggressive, nontheatrical behaviors. According to Gould, such behaviors promote a more ideal life of the spirit.

The equal voices of a contrapuntal texture typify a gesture that expresses the "anonymity dynamic." Gould held that within the anonymity milieu one can focus on the spiritually transcendent. Any narcissistic preoccupation is replaced by a transcendent conscience, which is rooted in a moral code that is above an individual's ego.

The energy of contrapuntal textures feels endless, and thus, suggests the infinite. Counterpoint can generate a contemplative sense of repose that for Gould is not a lack of energy, but rather, the product of an internal metamorphosis: the amalgam of ecstasy and reason (Gould, 1984b).

Gould's preoccupation with contrapuntal imagery could be linked with the way the "right-brained" mode perceives time to be nonlinear or nonsequential. Contrapuntal layers are simultaneous and undermine the notion of linearity. Their nonsequentiality imitates Eastern traditions of spirituality, which feature the mystical. To be nonsequential frees one to take a wholistic, harmonic approach to the inner and outer life. In this regard, Gould's metaphorical mind stresses spiritual health though a contrapuntal, wholistic approach.

Finally, to think contrapuntally means to synthesize complex events into a unifying vision. Translated into moral terms, making simple the complex is a way of creatively knowing and comprehending reality that fosters self-actualization. It represents a personal wholeness in that every note has an interrelated past, present, and future.

Contrapuntal imagery is also a metaphor for the realization that historical chronology is not important spiritually. Gould would most likely agree with Gabriel Moran's statement, "Everything is somehow connected to everything else, and what the human will calls end at any moment is not a termination point but a way of being in the continuing movement of history" (Moran, 1987, p. 40).

IMAGES OF GOING NORTH

Another metaphor that signals a moral message in Gould's work is the image of going north. In his media project entitled "The Idea of North," Gould challenged the artist to struggle, to venture upward, to wage war against the so-called natural and its limitations. In short, to adopt a transnatural morality of music that fosters growth of the human spirit.

The image of going north metaphorically demonstrates that it is not easy to follow such a path. Very often going north involves isolation, moving into the unknown, grappling with inner conflicts of values and living an ascetical, puritanical life. But hopefully, new life meanings and a revitalized way of being emerges out of the self-imposed ordeal (Gould, 1967–1968).

MODEL OF MORALITY FOR THE MUSICAL ARTIST

Both images, "contrapuntal textures" and "going north," speak a powerful language of morality for the musician. Gould emphasized that musicians should seek to fulfill their human potential through responsibility to their self, and then, to the world. The model Gould presented is primarily a framework for the musician to become a creative, articulate artist who is fulfilled in a vocation that fosters self-actualization.

Gould (1978e) wrote that society as a whole can improve only if the individual members, including the musical artist, are conscious of their personal and social responsibility to modify their private attitudes accordingly. It is the moral responsibility of the artist to engage in artistic activity that is aimed at the betterment of humanity.

Responsibility to oneself means the development of attitudes by which the musician can draw insights from inner truth rather than superimposed, artificial norms. In short, Gould was advocating self-knowledge and truthful self-expression based on that knowledge. This, in turn, supports the development of personal wholeness in the musical artist. It is a kind of wholeness that can be achieved only when a person is aware of and receptive to the innermost self (Sinetar, 1986). The musical artist is not fragmented but emotionally and spiritually unified because inner and outer lives are in harmony.

Whether he was conscious of it or not, Gould's work promoted what Sinetar (1986) called the genuine task of human existence, namely, the advancement of wholeness or self-actualization. Gould chose to be a marginal person in order to gain a wider perspective. What higher moral good is there than a person achieving the fundamental purpose of a life?

Gould unconditionally labored to achieve wholeness and upheld the idea that obedience to the voice of personal inspiration was essential for the musically honest artist. There was no room for compromise with external pressures for artistic judgments.

Thus, Gould wrote that the musician should dispense with the "yoke of respectability" (Gould, 1976d). In his own life he turned the expressive conventions, the respectable artistic standards of his day on their head because he responded to the deeper, moral levels of his being (Cott, 1984). He contended that the artificial symbols of status and competitiveness promulgated by society are obstacles to the truth (Gould, 1967). Gould intuitively knew that the self-actualizing individual must detach experientially from the conventions of the outside world in order to know the inner truth (Sinetar, 1986).

Gould rejected worldly conventions not for the sake of novelty but for the sake of achieving the moral good of his personal wholeness. He understood that being locked in cultural affectations is being in moral bondage. Robbins wrote in this regard, ". . . the cultural commandments that keep me from knowing myself as an artist also perpetuate injustice in the world" (Robbins, 1985).

Gould knew that sensitive regard for moral issues often involves abandoning comfortable life-styles in favor of social and self transcendence. To be socially and personally transcendent means abandoning old secure ways in favor of moving into uncharted spiritual waters. It means achieving emotional independence from societal influences and then experiencing a mystical, nonegoistical sense of self (Sinetar, 1986). These ideas were implemented by Gould (1976e) for the musician in that he advocated that music should not be reduced to a level of self-serving activity. He rejected applause as an external, shallow at best, public manifestation that detracts from the real purpose and value in art.

He suggested that the musician avoid extroverted, virtuosic theatrics that are self-serving and exhibitionistic (Gould, 1953). Finally, he categorized aggression as psychologically limiting behavior. Aggression focuses the attention of the artist on worldly successes rather than artistic ideas. A nonaggressive attitude would help to promote art as a humanly transcendent experience, which Gould (1974b) considered to be a superior spiritual good.

Gould wrote that it is far superior behavior for the musical artist to let go of egoistic interests than to pursue superficial, self-seeking interests. Gould opposed ego gratification in art because he reverenced art as something beyond pedestrian pursuits, something above the individual.

THE ECSTATIC VISION

Gould (1962e, 1983a) proposed that efforts to achieve ecstatic or peak moments should be substituted for shallow showmanship. He affirmed that the real purpose of art is the continual, lifelong creation of a state of wonder and serenity. The highest mission of morality is to remove ourselves from ourselves and achieve a state of ecstasy. In order to make such a claim he probably sensed that when we become ecstatic, we become aware of the divine in all of life (Robbins, 1985).

The ecstatic vision is the center of the self-actualized person. It is the peak experience of self-wholeness and actualization (Maslow, 1971). Gould was sensitive to the transformation power of the ecstatic moment. Sinetar explained that "During these moments the self, the ego (one's separateness) disappears, melts, as the individual fuses experientially with the object of perception: the cosmos or nature, his work . . ." (Sinetar, 1986, p. 6). Gould (1984b) considered the cultivation of a state of ecstasy to be the ultimate achievement of creativity.

Gould, as a self-transcendent, stressed the transformative approach to life rather than theoretical playing with ideas. Like other transcendents, he considered spiritual activity to be the dominating life-force inseparable from other activity. Gould's work reflects Sinetar's description of the self-transcendent wanting "an altered way of seeing and hearing. This necessitates . . . an obliteration of ego interests, bodily concerns, self-serving behaviors and irresponsible narcissism" (Sinetar, 1986, p. 83).

In summary, it could be said that Gould viewed art not

only as an end in itself but as a way to develop a deeply transformed inner-moral life. He imagined, as did Gabriel Moran, that "Genuine religious experience and great art are morality, not in what they prescribe or in the messages they deliver, but in simply being themselves, in being responses to a deeper level of being" (Moran, 1987, p. 52).

Gould knew, as did Dahlhaus (1983), that a separation of morality from aesthetics is futile. Thus, he offers an original course of thought for the philosophy of music that strongly links music to morality. He illustrates a way music can potentially foster a modern, transnatural morality of creative openness.

Gould surprises us with penetrating depths beyond the commonly assumed one-dimensionality of music. His supreme spiritual norm for music was, as Hans Kung wrote, ". . . not conformity to tradition, not novelty or actuality, but humanity: a humanity grounded, protected and secretly secure in divinity" (Kung, 1981, p. 50).

A SOCIOLOGY OF MUSIC

THE RELATIONSHIP OF MUSIC TO SOCIETY

Gould's social philosophy of music is linked very closely with his moral considerations. He advocated the existence of an important relationship between music and society. Unlike his ideas for a morality of music, Gould's thought for a social philosophy can be compared to several leading theories of music presented in chapter 3.

MARXIST AESTHETICS AND GOULD

There are several parallels between Gould's approach to the significance of music to society and Marxist aesthetics. Adorno (1967) claimed musical meaning or significance in that it results from intrinsic value as well as extramusical connections, like music's power for moral transformation. Music is referential for the Marxist in that its full meaning incorporates extramusical phenomena (Reimer, 1970). Gould's writings fully concur with this position.

Marxist aesthetic views music as a serious endeavor because music possesses the power to transform consciousness and work for the betterment of humanity (Johnson, 1984). Gould (1976a) likewise proposed that music should be used for the betterment of society.

Ballantine (1984) wrote that art is a mirror of society's social dynamics. Adorno (1973) offered an example of this when he wrote that the breakdown of tonality in the twentieth century is a reflection of bourgeois society's progressive dissolution. Adorno proposed that any contradiction inherent in music could only be resolved if and when socioeconomic contradictions were ameliorated (Mertens, 1983). In "Anthology of Variation," Gould also imagined that art is an accurate reflection of the social dynamics of society.

Throughout his writings, Gould rejected the use of historical musicology as a definitive source for the current interpretation of music. He, as well as Adorno (1976), discounted the concept of definitive interpretations in music (Weitzman, 1971).

Adorno (1973, 1976) declared that art's most dangerous enemy is a preoccupation with historical chronology in order to extract meanings. Gould (1964b) wrote that we should not employ historical chronology to judge a work's value. Rather, one should go to the work itself for its meanings.

Gould (1984b) criticized the critics for claiming to know the truth of a musical performance. Similarly, Adorno (1967) demystified the critic's authority as emanating from a higher objectivity than other listeners. Adorno considered that all listeners, including critics, are faced with similar problems of meaning and evaluation.

Like Adorno (1973) Gould favored Schoenberg's art over Stravinsky's work. Gould (1984b) thought Stravinsky lacked spiritual depth in his work. Adorno believed Schoenberg reflected the cultural progress of his times and was more genuinely artistic than Stravinsky for that reason. He also argued that Stravinsky's art ignored the cultural dialectic of his time, and thus, left a sterile, vacuous art.

Gould's sociological thought departs from Marxist ideas in the following ways. Gould (1964b, 1983a) contended that publicly auditioned musics are a vehicle of mass culture (e.g., Muzak possesses positive value for the musical development of the listener). The listener could automatically accumulate a vast vocabulary of musical clichés that could serve as the foundation for a wide listening repertoire. Marxists, such as Adorno and Horkheimer, scorned the culture industry's ability to reach people with propagandized media (DaSilva et al., 1984; Cott, 1984).

Unlike the practice in several socialist states, Gould (1964b) wrote that social consciousness should not be linked to social regulatory agencies. Instead, he maintained that social consciousness should be linked to one's pursuit of the spiritual perfection of the self. Personal, spiritual freedom was paramount in Gould's writings. He did not accept a culture that limits or tightly controls an artist's creativity.

Unlike Marxist predilection, Gould did not promote class struggle. Music was socially significant for Gould because of its potential to better humanity on a spiritual level. Freedom was an issue of spiritual, inner struggles for Gould. Although a political dimension can arise from such process, Gould did not address this level.

GOULD AND OTHER THEORIES

Gould differed from Meyer (1979, 1967) in that Meyer rejected the notion that music can humanize. And yet, Schantz (1983) wrote that Meyer's work leads to a contemplative view of art and self-realization. Since Gould's understanding of a morality and sociology of music were heavily contingent upon personal (spiritual) development, in this sense, Gould and Meyer were in congruence. The artist's perfectability encompasses moral, and consequently, social, ramifications.

Lippman (1977), although a modified formalist, suggested that the structures found in music reflect humanity's sociohistorical nature. There is some similarity of this thought to Gould's approach that gives weight to the formal properties of music but also recognizes extramusical connections.

Reimer (1970) also wrote that the absolute expressionist viewpoint supports the idea that musical meaning embodies a relationship of music to life. Musical meaning is both intrinsic and extrinsic to the musical composition. Although the author has not found explicit discussions of music's relationship to society in expressionistic literature, it is implied in Reimer's overview explanation of contemporary aesthetic theories. It is also reminiscent of Gouldian thought.

Phenomenological methodology as read in Ferrara (1978, 1984) places music within a sociological context when ontological or "world" explication is employed. However, such descriptions are not social or moral prescriptions for the betterment of humanity, and that is where they diverge from Gould's thought. Gould offered a clear path for spiritual development and its social ramifications.

Gould's ideas closely paralleled John Cage's view of contemporary music in that both Cage and Gould espoused the dissolution of the separation of art and life. With the disappearance of the dialectical link between form and content, the historical reference of a piece disappears. It is substituted by an absolute reality of the immediate phenomenal experience (Mertens, 1983).

A paradise of innocence prevails in both Gould's and Cage's puritanical Protestant roots. Their denunciation of contemporary sociocultural dynamics could be interpreted as leading to a kind of creed of nonactivity. On the other hand, both Cage and Gould carried forward their aesthetic projects to an ethical one where the historical, ontological duality of life and art is abandoned in favor of an ecstatic attitude that ultimately fosters transcendence and historical indifference.

Mertens wrote concerning Cage's music, ". . . unlike dialectical music [it] is no longer a 'representation of life' but the immediate genesis of life" (Mertens, 1983, p. 118). The traditional development found in historically grounded music has been replaced by both Gould and Cage with metamorphosis without end. Mertens (1983) called this an ecstatic process of pure libidinal activity that may indicate a kind of psychological regression.

In chapter 5, the author outlined Gould's views concerning status-hierarchy, professional specialization, and the roles of composer/performer/listener and institutions. These views show that he re-created the world by pointing out that the emphasis and custom of certain musical practices detracts from the real purpose of art: the creative development of one's spirituality.

Gould questioned the conventional status-hierarchy of the music world like no other musician-philosopher. This is true because he studied musical society from a spiritual, existential perspective. Prominent musicians like Sessions (1971), Copland (1959), Hindemith (1961), and Stravinsky (1947) discussed the roles of the composer, performer, listener only within the context of conventional wisdom, namely, formalist practice.

Foss (1976) briefly mentioned the trend in contemporary music to bring the composer closer to the performer by sharing some of the creative role with the performer. He omitted, as did many other music commentators, a critical analysis of the resultant status-hierarchy and its implications for society. Gould (1964b) alone attempted to question and offer insights for change in the roles and relationships of composers, performers, and listeners. He argued that the status-hierarchy is unnatural and only promotes false relationships.

Gould probed deeply into the composer's aesthetic functioning. He purported that composers should be willing to step out of their chronological time. They make richer their time by being eternally individualistic. Composers should also crystallize physical and spiritual experiences through artistic expression. (Gould especially favored spiritual qualities for contemplative expression.)

Gould presented the following as rationale for composers to accept multiple authorship: Anonymity is created with multiple authorship; Multiple authorship thwarts aggressive behavior; Individual opinion is redefined; Multiple authorship weakens the dominance of participants in the sociomusical hierarchy; Privacy is facilitated through multiple authorship.

Gould, likewise, offered a sociomusical model for the ideal role of the artist/performer: The artist should accept being in a state of flux; The performer should facilitate the listening to spiritual qualities inherent in the music. The performer should assume an ecstatic attitude when performing; never be mechanical; project individuality, purpose, and conviction; possess faith in the unknown in order to free potential possibilities for interpretation. The artist should be willing to sacrifice personal comfort in order to achieve musical and spiritual integrity; utilize imagery as the core of his or her performance; and finally, analysis should assume great importance for the performer.

The model above is not only autobiographical of Gould's attitudes about performance practice, it also demonstrates his understanding of the creative growth process. Chapter 7 offers further explication of Gould's intuition of the creative process.

Finally, Gould gave a perspective of the ideal listener. He predicted that a new kind of listener is emerging. The thinking listener is able to bracket out sounds in order to understand them in a phenomenological way. The future listener is one who, at the center of the performance problem, should assume, as should the artist, an ecstatic attitude.

AN EPISTEMOLOGY OF MUSIC

An epistemology is both a guide to constructing new knowledge and analyzing the knowledge in existing literature. It is a structure of knowledge that explains the parts and their relationships. It examines facts, interpretations, explanations, generalizations, value and knowledge claims, theories, and concepts in order to arrive at a structure of knowledge (Gowin and Dyason, 1984).

Knowing in music transcends the narrow view that only

verifiable knowledge is real. Musical knowledge involves an understanding of both the elements from which music comes, namely, a theory of music and the complex effects music exerts upon the listener (Reid, 1941).

WHAT KINDS OF KNOWLEDGE DOES MUSIC REVEAL?

What did Glenn Gould (1964b) mean when he wrote that music reveals emotional knowledge? Since he did not explicitly discuss the full meaning of emotions in his writings, one can only speculate about his intent. Is Gould's concept of expression in music linked to theories that claim music expresses actual emotions? Gould's emphasis of intuitive knowledge warrants a comparison of his thought on this subject with expressionism.

Benedetto Croce (1970) proposed that intuition is always an emotion, and art is the expression of emotion. Croce's equation, intuition = expression, is the prototype of expressionist theory. A possible argument might follow that since Gould professed that music is a vehicle for revelation (possibly meaning intuition) and intuition is always an emotion (Croce), then music potentially expresses actual emotions. The weakness of this line of reasoning rests on the fact that we are not certain of Gould's meaning of the word *revelation*.

Does Langer's (1942) theory of a formal analogy between music and emotions apply to Gould? Her theory demonstrates the possibility that music discloses the knowledge of insight in emotional life.

Gould very often used ambiguous expressions (e.g., personal inspiration, intuition, ecstasy, and revelation) in his writings. These utterances point to the fact that his thought leans towards nondiscursive, rather than discursive, modes of expression. Perhaps Gould's (1964b) system of emotional reference is virtual, as developed by Langer, and not actual, as set forth by expressionists. Like Langer (1942), who defended nondiscursive forms of knowledge, Gould (1958a) considered that an artist's intuition is important knowledge embodied in an art work. Gould

(1968c) further wrote that the structural forms of the music reveal intuitive intelligence through inspiration.

Music unfolds a rationality that is cognitive, nondiscursive, and necessary for the human spirit (Langer, 1953). Gould concurred with Langer in that music discloses artistic insight that is not mystical but intuitive (Wade, 1965). Music reveals a knowledge of universal concepts that transcends individual consciousness.

Gould emphasized the importance of music's formal aspects (i.e., knowledge of traditional harmony, analysis methodology, and knowledge of contrapuntal techniques). Gould (1958a) wrote that through the study of music we can know an openness to spontaneous structure expansion within the music. In other words, we can know music unfolding itself. Gould's thought also incorporated Gurney's (1880) principle that music informs the person of unknown things through its expressive form.

Gould parted with the traditional formalist position (e.g., Stravinsky, 1947; Hindemith, 1961; Lippman, 1977) of those who claim that music has no external reference, in that he went further and assigned referential meaning to music (i.e., moral, social, and epistemological dimensions). Gould (1980, 1964b) envisioned music to be a conduit for personal revelation. It is through the music that we can know ourselves. We can also know the "world" through the music's metaphorical connotations. Thus, Gould's epistemology of music is three-pronged; music reveals itself (formalist); music reveals the person (expressionist); music reveals the world (referentialist).

Gould's tri-part musical knowledge is reminiscent of the phenomenologist's reflective process as developed by Lawrence Ferrara. Ferrara (1984) unfolded a three-tiered epistemological construct, based on Heideggerian thought, that yielded the phenomenological method when applied to a musical composition. The syntactical, semantic, and ontological elements of meaning emerge when Ferrara's procedure is employed. The syntactical level uncovers the music itself; the semantic level divulges referential factors; the ontological level unmasks the world set in sound.

Gould's construct of musical knowledge shows similarity

to Ferrara's model in that music reveals itself (syntax); music reveals the person (semantic); and music reveals the world (semantic and ontological). The last chapter of this book focuses on ways in which music reveals the person.

Finally, there is no evidence in Gould's writings that indicates any strong interest in or similarity to semiotic approaches, as found in Coker (1972) and Nattiez (1975), and subsequent iconic theories of knowledge.

WHAT METHOD SHOULD WE USE TO KNOW A MUSICAL WORK?

Gould (1956b) reported that music discloses itself. Therefore, one should connect or "presence" oneself to the musical work. This attitude again shows a similarity to the phenomenological method as purported by Ferrara (chapter 3). The fact that Gould advocated that one should "presence" oneself to the music is phenomenological in countenance.

Initially the listener, if applying phenomenological methodology, suspends all judgments (all awareness of the world) and enters into the musical work. The composition is then permitted to disclose itself because the listener is open to it. Gould, like the phenomenologist, stressed the necessity of going back to the work itself in order to really know it.

He repeatedly rejected the approach to music that relies on explanatory commentary as a source for understanding the music. Gould stressed that music reveals itself, first and foremost, by one's experiencing it.

WHAT IS THE RELATIONSHIP OF THE PERFORMER
TO MUSICAL KNOWLEDGE?

Gould asserted that the performer's knowledge should be based on mental imagery (Dubal, 1984). Sessions (1971) expressed a similar view when he wrote that the performer's task is "to apply his imagination to discovering the musical gestures inherent in the composer's text, and then, to reproducing them according to his own lights; that is with fullest participation on his own part" (Sessions, 1971, p. 78). However, Gould's concept of mental imagery projects beyond finding the means to reproduce the composer's ideas in a score. Gould's mental imagery stresses the spiritual, intuitional side to music . He encouraged one to delve into the music to discover new meanings that, perhaps, transcend even the composer's concept of the music.

The performer's knowledge of music should come from within and can complement the composer's view (Gould, undated, media transcript, "Glenn Gould interviewed by Bernard Asbell"). This view is sharply in opposition to Stravinsky's (1947) idea that performers should obey the letter of the score above all other considerations. Stravinsky believed that knowledge should be based on the text of the music. He wrote, "The sin against the spirit of the work always begins with a sin against its letter and lends to the endless follies which an ever flourishing literature in the worst taste does its best to sanction" (Stravinsky, 1947, p. 129).

Stravinsky further wrote,

> The secret of perfection lies above all in his consciousness of the law imposed upon him by the work he is performing. And here we are back at the great principle of submission that we have so often invoked in the course of our lessons.
>
> This submission demands a flexibility that itself requires, along with technical mastery, a sense of tradition and, commanding the whole, an aristocratic culture that is not merely a question of acquired learning. (Stravinsky, 1947, pp. 132–133).

Gould and Stravinsky are worlds apart in that Gould recommended that the artistic decisions of the performer can complement and even enlighten the composer. Stravinsky unyieldingly claimed supreme artistic power and control for the composer. His tone treats the performer like an artistic robot for the composer's egoistical whim, rather than displaying a humanist's concern for the spiritual growth of the performer.

Finally, Gould (1980b) warned that the performer

should practice for ideas rather than for achieving a physical connection with the keyboard. The performer's tactile knowledge should be spontaneous and no amount of academic systematization can really help the performer to achieve a true technique. Gould sensed the danger of a mechanical approach to performance. Hindemith (1961) shared the same reservation about performers losing the freshness of interpretation when their playing becomes mechanical and routine. He wrote, "Routine replaces enthusiasm, feelings lose their genuineness, endless repetitions of the same restricted number of facts create an atmosphere of fictitious truth" (Hindemith, 1961, p. 168).

7. CONCLUSIONS FOR A PHILOSOPHY OF MUSIC EDUCATION

INTRODUCTION

Leonhard (1972) thought that music education's contribution to general education should be better understood. He suggested that research be carried out to discover what kind of impact music has on the education of the person. He further stated that standards of value, based on synthetic treatments of the foremost aesthetic theories, should be formulated for the development of sound educational objectives for musicians and music education programs. It is through the application of these values that music is empowered to contribute to the person's ultimate self-actualization and fulfillment.

Gould's writings are in congruence with Leonhard's notion, in that music can influence human growth and development. This author attempts to illustrate in this chapter how Gould's thought can possibly impact the development of a philosophy of music education by advocating ways in which the musician can attain self-realization and subsequent fulfillment. (In this context, the word "musician" means one who engages throughout a lifetime in the pursuit of learning [knowing] music.)

Throughout this study we discover that Gould's ideas assume axiological significance and are a step towards a theoretical framework (a synthetic construct) within which the musician can discover levels of personal and interpersonal meanings. His perceptions engender discussions about important musical and educational matters. Generalizations can be formulated and speculative interpretations can be extended to practical educational implementation through the use of the synthetic construct implied in Gould's writings.

As was stated earlier, the seemingly disparate statements in Gould's written output can acquire a broad, significant meaning if interpreted in terms of creative openness and human growth. Other musicians, acting as philosopher-educators, discuss music's value for human growth. Few attempt this task through an explication of spiritual growth values. Gould appears to be unique in implying that self-actualization through music is a path to spiritual fulfillment.

Self-actualization is not a new concept to music education. Its application is well documented from the 1960's to the present in American music education. What is unique in Gould's writing is that he persistently links self-actualization through music with a spiritual (moral) dimension.

Just as morality is at the apex of Gould's model for a philosophy of music, ideas for human growth are at the apex of his model for a philosophy of music education. Human growth involves all the actions, activities, and processes necessary for the fulfillment of a person's potential.

All too often, leading the life of a musician can be a frustrating experience. Gould presents a way in which the musician can transcend socioartistic alienation and lead a satisfyingly creative life. Gould offered a human values oriented approach to education in which human fulfillment is achieved through interaction with the music. Music is experienced as a catalyst by which the musician can ultimately achieve self-actualization, transcendence, and spiritual fulfillment. The following questions arise: How is this accomplished? And what are the insights Gould presented for the musician's spiritual growth? The answer to these questions rests in an examination of the relationship of Gould's ideas, Abraham Maslow, and music education.

GOULD, MASLOW, AND MUSIC EDUCATION

One sees in Glenn Gould's writings that music education is thought important not only for producing artists but for turning out artists who are better people. Lewis (1972) documented that Abraham Maslow was of like mind in his view that the primary function of education is to facilitate the personal growth of the student.

Lewis (1972) wrote that Maslow developed a theory of basic human needs in his writings. These needs are hierarchical, going from the lowest level (biological needs) to higher needs (safety, love, esteem, desire to know, desire to understand, desire to belong) to the highest needs (aesthetic needs in the form of truth, beauty, and goodness).

The satisfaction of needs enables self-actualization and the full development of human potential. If these needs are not met then the realization of human potential is impossible. Gould intuitively understood this in regard to the musician. There are parallels found in Maslow's humanistic psychology and Gould's model for the development of a philosophy of music education. Lewis (1972) wrote that Maslow "studied the very best in human nature and thereby focused on the height of human achievement" (Lewis, 1972, p. 28). It is fully documented in this book that Gould did likewise by challenging himself and others to wholistic excellence.

The five principal tenets of Maslow's humanistic psychology are self-actualization, peak experiences, the hierarchy of needs, creativity, and spiritual values. This list could easily be transposed as the foundation of Gould's philosophy of music education.

Self-actualization can be translated as self-discovery of inner identity in Gould's thought. Peak experiences can be equated with Gould's preoccupation with the ecstatic condition. The hierarchy of human needs, presented above, is also found in Gould's creation-centered spirituality. And like Maslow, creativity and spiritual values are key considerations in Gould's thought for music education.

INTRINSIC EDUCATION

Gould advocated an intrinsic approach to education in which the teacher's role is more passive than what is traditionally the case in American pedagogical practice. Gould (1980b, 1984b) proposed that the teacher pose lead questions in the instructional process that are sensitive to the individual's unique intellectual needs. The teacher should not brainwash the students. It is far more advantageous in learning situations that the teacher be passive.

Lewis described Maslow's similar viewpoint found in his book, *The Farther Reaches of Human Nature*. Lewis wrote,

> The implication from Maslow is that the teacher with the humanistic goal would allow a more intrinsic mode of learning to prevail. The humanistic teacher would adopt a more taoistic philosophy, a philosophy that stresses asking rather than telling and one that would be more non-interfering and non-controlling. Taoistic teaching stresses receptiveness and passiveness by the teacher rather than activeness and forcefulness. (Lewis, 1972, p. 35)

Maslow (1971) stated that intrinsic education permits glimpses into the infinite, into ultimate value. Gould, likewise, wrote that intrinsic education promotes the highest values in humanity since the student is encouraged to glean personal truth as a result of self-introspection and discovery.

It is interesting to note that in intrinsic education peak experiences (Gould's ecstasy) simultaneously become motivational and a reward (Lewis, 1972). Ecstasy becomes the key ingredient of a biofeedback cycle of stimulation and satisfaction.

Each writer, in his work, promoted the fulfillment of human potential. Maslow called the discovery of identity (i.e., potentially possible through intrinsic education) self-actualization. Gould emphasized in his writings that the musician should search for personal identity as a necessary step to personal fulfillment. Maslow asserted the necessity for an individual to experience self-actualization in order to reach fulfillment.

Finally, Maslow (1971) wrote that all self-actualizing people exercise creativity. Creativity and the dispositions that promote creativity are, therefore, paramount for the self-actualized person. It is advisable to examine Gould's ideas connected with creativity in order to illustrate further parallels with Maslow's views.

CREATIVITY

It is fully documented in this book that Gould outlined in his work dispositions that facilitate creativity in the musician. Robbins (1985) cites six similar stages of creativity:

Preparation (data gathering);
Frustration (a time of pain, confusion, chaos, and ambiguity);
Incubation (a time to trust that an insight will occur to help solve the problem, right-brained activity);
Illumination (the answer, feeling of rightness);
Elaboration (analytic, left-brained activity);
Communication (communication completes the creative process).

Gould's ideas for creativity present a striking parallel with the above-mentioned six stages of creativity. The reader is asked to recall what is documented in earlier chapters:

- Gould's belief that the ability to utilize ambiguity is a desirable trait in the musician (frustration);
- Gould's admonition that the musician should trust the truth of inner inspiration (incubation);
- Gould's insistence that the feeling of rightness is the supreme norm for creative musicians (illumination);
- Gould's assertion that analysis should play an important role in music making (elaboration);
- Gould's dedication to morally responsible social interaction and communication of the artist and all involved in music (communication).

There are other parallels in examining the characteristics of creativity found in Gould's thought with Maslow, Robbins, and Sinetar. Maslow (1971) cited inspiration and improvisation as two major aspects of creativity. He cited "primary creativity" (i.e., the inspirational phase, the unconscious, the source of new discovery, novel ideas, and improvisation) as the most important form of creativity for music education.

Gould's work consistently addressed intuition, revelation, and openness to infinite creative possibilities. These are aspects of "primary creativity" and the fact that the creative process is more important than the perfection of the product.

Robbins (1985) wrote that creativity leads to spiritual fulfillment in that the artist's journey is also the mystic's path. Both artist and mystic seek inner-centering and self-transcendence. In this regard, Robbins outlined the four paths of spiritual life: (1) the way of blessing (creativity seen as divine potential; each of us has an innate responsibility to foster creativity); (2) the way of emptiness or letting go of value systems around us in order to create a new vision; (3) the way of creativity (affirms ambiguity in the creative process; it is dialectical consciousness in which polarities carry possibilities of unity); (4) the way of transformation (is empowerment, prophetic, nonhierarchical, compassionate, joyful, humorous).

Gould's thought strongly resembles the above points. In chapters 5 and 6 it is documented that Gould untiringly worked towards creativity that was moral, personally and socially responsible, and reverential. He advocated absolute faithfulness to one's inner vision above outside influences and believed that negation and ambiguity were essential to creativity. Finally, he prophetically embraced nonhierarchical, compassionate, joyful, and humorous values.

Creativity flows *to* self-actualization and flows *from* self-actualization. It is recorded in chapter 6 that self-transcendence and social-transcendence are a part of this process, which Gould wrote of and tangibly practiced in his artistic life.

Self-transcendence involves an elevated moral sense; an experiencing the mystical; the ego is transcended and a person unites with work, object, or others. Social-

transcendence means "emotional independence or detachment from societal influences, even from other people
when necessary." Out of the self-imposed ordeal new
meanings emerge (Sinetar, 1986, p. 5).

Sinetar (1986) outlined six abilities that appear to
develop as a consequence of social-transcendence: to
recognize the self in the context of a truthful, world-view;
to control life's resources rather than being controlled by
them; to renounce things, status symbols, material goods,
conventional pressures; to tolerate more ambiguity; to
merge self and other interests; and to see more clearly what
needs to be done in a problem-solving situation.

The above characteristics describe both psychological
development (i.e., self-understanding, self-acceptance,
personal integration), and spiritual development (i.e.,
disappearance of self into transcendent aspects of reality,
letting go of ego interests). As has been clearly demonstrated Gould possessed and wrote extensively about both.
The reader must not lose sight of the potential implications
this can have for a philosophy of music education.

NEGATION

In a lecture delivered to the graduating class of 1964 of the
Royal Conservatory of Music, Toronto, Gould (1964a)
advanced the importance of relating all learning to its
relationship with negation. He felt that if we lose sight of
negation's relationship with our learned discoveries, our
creative capacity will be put in jeopardy. Negation stirs
invention like no other concept.

Robbins cited the Indian philosopher Krishnamurti
when she wrote, "The great Indian philosopher Krishnamurti also speaks of emptiness: 'It is only when there is
emptiness in ourself, not the emptiness of a shallow mind,
but the emptiness that comes with the total negation of
everything one has been and should be and will be'—it is
only in this emptiness that there is creation" (Robbins,
1985, p. 73).

Negation in creativity points to a Janusian way of

thinking (i.e., two or more opposites or antitheses are conceived simultaneously). Rothenberg (1979) wrote that some of the world's greatest creative achievements emanate from the tensions between opposites. The creator develops antithetical pieces and integrates them into a new creation. Negation, which points to ambiguity, is essential to the creative process (Robbins, 1985).

SPIRITUAL GROWTH AND FULFILLMENT

Gould believed the following qualities (extracted and synthesized from Gould's writings) promote spiritual growth and fulfillment for the musician: (1) Healthy self-esteem—develop attitudes that are not neurotic or narcissistic in the face of the plurality of musical and nonmusical forces (e.g., aesthetic, political, economic, and educational); (2) Realistic assessment of talents and expectations—assessment should be based on inner knowledge grounded in self-worth rather than values that emanate from outer endorsement (e.g., ego gratification from competitions, virtuosic display, awards); (3) Removal of mystery from performance field, deglorification and demystification of talent—this promotes looking "within" for the reality that music is intrinsically valuable, not for the power it can release for the performer; (4) Moral sensitivity—applied to the entire range of living, this is a reverence for life through self and social transcendence, creative openness; (5) Social responsibility—social justice by becoming ourselves; a dialectic between solitude and social interaction; (6) The cultivation of ecstasy.

Ecstasy, Spirituality, and Music Educatuion

Gould emphasized that cultivating a state of ecstasy is the nucleus of spiritual consciousness and development. He presented the following comments about ecstasy.

The ecstatic state frees one from oneself (Gould, 1977c). It is through the ecstatic musical experience that we learn and know beyond the surface of momentary musical expression. We probe into deeper levels of artistic and transcendent consciousness (Gould, 1973c). The highest mission of a superior morality is to remove ourselves from ourselves and achieve a state of ecstasy (Gould, 1983a).

Gould wrote, ". . . the ultimate achievement for 'creative opter-outers' is the cultivation of a state of ecstasy" (Gould, 1984b, p. 445). Ecstasy is the only "proper quest for the artist" (Gould, 1984b, p. 254). The quality of ecstasy should be a dimension of the performance phenomenon (Gould, 1978e). The performer who is ecstatic functions on the level of transcendence, the highest level of consciousness.

Before one can experience artistic ecstasy, one must engage in solitude (Gould, 1973d). The listener should assume an ecstatic attitude that is potentially shared with the performer and composer in a "web of inner awareness" (Payzant, 1978, p. 16). Gould further wrote, ". . . ecstasy is a commodity most purveyed by fugal situations" (Gould, 1984b, p. 150). The author asks the reader to examine the similarities of Gould's statements with the thought presented below.

As was mentioned earlier in this chapter, Maslow equated the ecstatic moment with peak experiences or moments of rapture. Sinetar wrote the following concerning the peak experience:

> Through the peak experience the individual gains an expanded view of himself and the world, is lifted "above" the world and his own limitations . . . in a way that resolves personality splits, contradictions and blocks to full functioning. (Sinetar, 1986, p. 94)

This "lifting up" of the self, this resolution of conflicts within the self, gives rise to the term transcendence, which means going beyond ordinary limits, or surpassing normal human experience (Sinetar, 1986).

Lewis wrote that

> The peak experience can be described as a moment in a person's life in which he is functioning at his best; a moment in which a person sees himself and the outer world

in perspective, an experience that has the ability to change the life of an individual. (Lewis, 1972, p. 40)

Lewis continued,

It is from the peak experience that an individual most easily learns his true identity, what values he should pursue, and what is going on inside himself. The peak experience is one way to teach self-actualization and self-identity. (Lewis, 1972, p. 40)

Peak experiences open people up to all kinds of possibilities. Through the peak experience a person's entire belief system can be altered. Since peak experiences are moments of illumination, insight that renews the world is gained. "The micro-macro web of the universe" is understood in a flash (Sinetar, 1986, p. 99). It is a time of great happiness, focus, total absorption, power, and freedom.

Robbins (1985) wrote that when we experience ecstatic moments we see beneath the surface. We see a world far more real than the world of ordinary consciousness. Leonard (1968) added the following about ecstasy and education. He stated that ecstasy was a remedy to reduce aggression. Since joy resides within the self, those who seek intrinsic happiness have no time or inclination for aggression. Ecstasy is not necessarily opposed to reason, but may even help to integrate and illuminate the relationship of society and educational systems. Ecstasy is not necessarily opposed to order, but may in fact help to redefine order in a more qualitative rather than quantitative way. Finally, ecstasy is not moral or immoral of itself, rather, it is a powerful ally for education.

Gould showed that music can be a facilitator, a conduit, to achieve the educationally valuable, transformative ecstatic experience. Through musical ecstasy one can instantaneously experience an expanded awareness of life beyond momentary musical expression.

Leonard wrote, "One of the first tasks of education, then, is to return man to himself; to encourage rather than stifle awareness, the so-called autonomous systems, to help

people become truly responsive and therefore truly responsible" (Leonard, 1968, p. 127). Awareness is a most
valuable state for education since it is an energy of
consciousness that allows us to focus on only what is
(Gallwey & Kriegel, 1977).

Ecstasy liberates one from self-limitation or those parts
of the self that limit one from achieving human potential.
Human potential is usually greater than imagined (Leonard, 1968). Ecstasy feeds human potential in order to
possibly achieve accelerated learning, internal imagery,
problem solving, changing value systems, and other educational phenomena.

A SPIRITUAL GROWTH AXIOLOGY

Robbins arrived at five growth values for the development
of spirituality from the work of Yankelovich, Schumaker,
Dodson, Gray, and Ferguson:

1) Comprehensive reverence—the sense of the sacred in
   all life.
2) A whole-systems ethic—stresses interconnectedness;
   it is the moral responsibility of the artist working for
   the betterment of humanity.
3) Non-hierarchical values—anticompetition, antiag-
   gression, nonegoistical.
4) Voluntary simplicity—the rejection of worldly
   conventions; detachment from symbols of status.
5) Individual responsibility—self-sufficiency; entrepre-
   neurship; conservation; health-consciousness.

Each of the five growth values above is strongly reflected
in Gould's work. In addition, Robbins (1985) cited five
more growth values coined by D. Yankelovich. Gould's
work easily fits within this model.

1) Voluntary simplicity—Gould's work reflects the ideal
   of simplicity.

CHART OF COMPARATIVE VALUES

Paradigm for Musician	Paradigm of Protection Values	Paradigm of Growth Values
1) openness to spontaneity (Gould, 1958b; 1980b)	1) safety	1) spontaneity—willingness to risk
2) willingness to endure discomfort in the pursuit of artistic truth (Gould, 1984b)	2) comfort	2) meaning—willingness to confront life, including pain and contradiction
3) divergence from accepted musical interpretations in favor of personal insight and inspiration (Gould, 1980b)	3) image	3) authenticity—willingness to diverge from cultural norms
4) inner confidence (Gould, 1976a)	4) self-control	4) self-knowledge—self-understanding and trust
5) opposition to ego gratification in music (Gould, 1974b)	5) ego defenses	5) vulnerability—acknowledgment of weaknesses and emergence of strengths
6) artist in constant state of flux (Gould, 1972)	6) permanence	6) potential—recognition of flux dynamics of life
7) acceptance of the uncertainty of creativity in order to cultivate invention (Gould, 1984b)	7) information	7) insight—eagerness to learn
8) Gould's written output stresses the limitless spiritual potential for music/musicians	8) adjustment	8) aspiration—belief in human potential
9) shared authorship of composer and others	9) power over others	9) power with others—cooperation

Paradigm for Musician	*Paradigm of Protection Values*	*Paradigm of Growth Values*
10) connecting to others through music (especially via recordings) the musician can achieve a unique closeness with the listener in recording (Gould, 1980c)	10) feeling superior to others	10) feeling connected to others—identity with human traits
11) musician should frame morally and socially responsible values (Gould, 1984b)	11) freedom from responsibility	11) freedom in responsibility— sense of personal power

2) Decline in competitiveness—Gould takes a non-competitive, nonhierarchical stance.
3) Ethic of commitment—Gould is committed to the highest artistic and spiritual standards throughout his writings.
4) Reverential thinking—Gould lived a transnatural, reverential life and reflected this in his writings.
5) Creation of community—Gould sought direct communication in the most personal way through recording, thus creating community.

The chart on pp. 183–184 is a comparison of Gould's paradigm for growth in the musician, protection values, and a paradigm of growth values developed by Marilyn Ferguson. Take note of the close parallel between Gould's ideas and Ferguson's model.

IMPLICATIONS FOR MUSIC EDUCATION

What are the implications from Gould's writings for a philosophy of music education?
    Gould implied that

1) music education should capitalize on intuitive modes of learning;
2) unself-conscious knowing should be stressed in educational settings;
3) music education should never be marked by competition;
4) the music educator has a unique role in instilling inner values for the student;
5) music education should be concerned with the end of art;
6) music education interpenetrates life;
7) music education is lifelong and does not end with the influence of "formal" institutions;
8) music education should be geared towards the development of the whole person (i.e., spiritually and socially integrated).

INTUITIVE MODES OF LEARNING

Wholistic knowledge relies on intuition. Intuition is a basic epistemological premise in Gould's philosophy of music and music education. He shared this view with Langer who claimed that intuition is "the psychological activity which makes the arts a mode of knowing, a universe of discourse" (Wade, 1965, p. 176).

Goldberg wrote, ". . . intuition would be favored by a combination of low arousal and high alertness—a calm, wakeful receptive state with relatively little mental noise to interfere with the input of the intuitive mode" (Goldberg, 1983, p. 136). This sounds reminiscent of Gould's advice for the performer to cultivate an attitude of contemplation (a state of alert openness and calm).

The nonverbal, nonsequential modes of knowing are very often attributed to the right brain only. In a normal person both hemispheres are in constant interaction (Goldberg, 1983). Gould implied a way to greater integration and collaboration of the two hemispheres of the brain through his advancement of intuitive and analytical thinking.

As was mentioned earlier, much of Gould's writing is an

autobiographical account of his inner life. It could also be considered an insight or model of mind: a description of the mind of artistic genius. It is a hierarchical model of mind that resembles Goldberg's description, "Each deeper level would be more stable, more universal, less restricted by space and time, and closer to the truth, since pure consciousness is silent, all-pervading, beyond time and space, and eternal" (Goldberg, 1983, p. 138). Finally, in intuitive mode the steps are neither conscious nor deliberate. This leads to a discussion on unself-conscious knowing.

Unself-conscious Knowing

Unself-conscious knowing is a breakthrough stage of concentration: a process of letting go. Your mind enters the world of pure experience. Total connections of action, thinking, awareness, and doing are integrated. One functions in wholistic awareness (Gallwey & Kriegel, 1977).

Gould promoted such a high degree of wholistic concentration in that he did not believe one should verbalize the physical processes of performance, and he advocated that learning music with ambient noise present frees the brain to center on inner imagination. It frees the brain to operate on "automatic mode" (i.e., to function in a meditative state [alpha brain waves]). Silva called this the optimum state for creativity and learning (Silva, 1977).

In Gould's performance practice his incessant humming and singing may have helped him to shift mental gears to the alpha state of consciousness: a nondiscursive state conducive to "presencing" himself to the music.

Unself-conscious modes of knowing relate to Gould's claim that he could teach everything about the piano to a receptive student in about a half-hour. Perhaps by employing these modes Gould was on to a way for accelerated learning in music. Silva (1977) called the alpha-meditative state an optimum learning environment conducive to accelerated learning.

Concerning unself-conscious knowing, Gallwey and Kriegel wrote,

The very quality of our daily experience depends on the development of this master skill. The quality of our concentration can make the difference between a life that is satisfying and alive and one that is incomplete and dull. Two skiers can stand atop the same mountain and one can be experiencing a transcendent beauty while the other is seeing just another mountain. The difference in the quality of their perceptions lies in the quality of their attention. (Gallwey & Kriegel, 1977, p. 182)

COMPETITIONS

Gould opposed the concept of competition for the following reasons: Originality is discouraged at competitions (Gould, 1966e); Competitions favor artists whose vision is less than ecstatic (Gould, 1984b); Test pieces in competitions usually emphasize technical prowess rather than artistic vision (Gould, 1966e); The vocabulary used in connection with competitions is aggressive in tone and gives evidence of individual feelings being repudiated; Imaginations and self-awareness are reduced to a minimum (Gould, 1974b); Juries are usually inadequate to the task of judging (Gould, 1984b).

There is a strong parallel in Gould's thought with educational existentialist, G. B. Leonard. Leonard (1968) wrote that competition produces close resemblance among the individuals involved. It creates standardization essential to high structure in society. People who lead unique, centered lives put traditional social structures out of balance.

It is clear that both Gould and Leonard were opposed to musicians seeking artistic validation from others. Gould sensed that searching for value outside oneself can lead the musician to paths of self-alienation. Leonard wrote in this regard that "Piling up honors, tangible or intangible, has had the effect of divorcing the student from his own feelings, his own being. A man's worth. . .is measured by things outside himself" (Leonard, 1968, pp. 121–122).

Leonard (1968) wrote that signs of success are measured

by symbol. Gould (1967d) rejected the symbols of competitiveness used in competitions as false measures for accomplishment. He abandoned the signs of achievement promulgated by society as misleading, dangerous, and judged that they lead away from rather than to the truth. Both Leonard (1968) and Gould (1978a) rejected competition because it almost always encourages aggression.

Gould believed it is necessary for the artist to be centered and in touch with inner awareness. He reacted to the attitude of competitive acquisition by advocating an intense feeling state leading to ecstasy in the artist. In addition, he promoted the artist to engage in the musical art work (phenomenological awareness), not historical, philosophical discussion.

The three ways Gould (1978a, 1978b, 1973c) suggested to circumvent competitive society are through technology, ecstasy, and anonymity.

THE MUSIC EDUCATOR

Gould (1984b) saw the music educator of his experiences as a threat to the student's learning. He imagined that students were kept in intellectual and artistic bondage by tutorial hierarchy; teachers who promote passivity in the student; teachers who offer too much gratuitous advice; indoctrination of learning institutions; and teachers who treat students as inferior people.

Gould (1980b, 1984b) believed, as an educator with existentialist leanings, that teachers should merely assist students to focus on the student's own, already existing, artistic powers. Students should pursue their own way to personal truth and development. In order to further this process the teacher should pose lead questions for the student's reflection.

Gould was critical of music educators, in general, because all too often they do not recognize the student's individuality. They offer large amounts of standardization neglecting personal creativity. Gould asserts that the teacher should be expansive and help the student to overcome, not create, self-limiting attitudes (e.g., low self-esteem, overdependence on the teacher).

Gould counseled that students should stand up to domineering teachers. Very often music students with fragile egos become victims of the artificial, distorted "worlds" of the teacher. Students need educators who will promote healthy mental wholeness and self-actualization. Educators should assist students to grow in spite of their own frustrations with the music profession (e.g., not adequately appreciated by society, low sociostatus, low self-esteem).

Gould would most likely concur with Leonard that "learning has to do with the response of the child, not with the presentation of the teacher" (Leonard, 1968, p. 108). Learning should be student-centered, not teacher-centered.

MUSIC EDUCATION AND THE END OF ART

Gould, as a futurist, wrote about "the spiritual good that ultimately will serve to banish art itself" (Gould, 1984b, pp. 446–447). Why should music education have a role in participating in its own obsolescence? The answer to that question is obvious in Gould's writings. Music should not be wrapped up in its own importance but always be conscious of its moral and spiritual ramifications.

Gould (1974b) imagined that music, as all art, is valuable only insofar as it fosters the spiritual growth of the individual. Since art has the potential to be destructive to the human spirit, it should be allowed to die in favor of the spiritual good.

Others expressed similar futuristic views about the end of art. Robbins, in quoting Henry Miller, wrote about a more benign picture of the future when "Art will one day disappear. But the artist will remain, and life itself will become not 'an art,' but art. . . . Once art is really accepted it will cease to be. It is only a substitute, a symbol language, for something which can be seized directly" (Robbins, 1985, p. 146).

Leonard expressed an identical view when he wrote that society will become art. He said, "It may turn out that the contemporary artist is engaged in the business of ending art, thereby helping us create an environment in which each individual life may be lived as a work of art" (Leonard, 1968, p. 98).

Robbins quoted Rank's futuristic comment that the artist must let go of art for higher reasons. She wrote, "Rank puts it in the most challenging terms: 'The creative type who can renounce this protection by art and can devote his whole creative force to life and the formation of life will be the first representative of the new human type' " (Robbins, 1985, p. 59).

EXISTENTIALISM

Gould advocated intrinsic education, heeding the truth of inner inspiration, letting go of traditional values, ecstasy, spirituality, intuitive modes of knowing, unself-conscious knowing, embracing negation, and the end of art. All of these share an existential vision for music education.

The existentialist believes that people who conform to values set outside of the self live inauthentic lives. Thus, nontraditional, self-sufficient choices are considered superior to choices that conform to traditional values. The choosing being is ultimately responsible for the consequences of his or her choices because the truth is mediated through personal meanings based on individual choices and actions.

Individual meanings are considered authentic only within a framework of total freedom. One's morality is also considered contingent upon the individual's needs, choices, and consequences. The teacher should consider the student to be a fellow searcher for truth. The teacher is to be a questioner, a prober in the educational process.

It is documented throughout this book that Gould brought together the ideas above specifically for the musician. In reflecting on his own mind, Gould opened up a way to spiritual development for the musician.

FINAL COMMENTS

Do Gould's ideas offer any insight for a philosophy of music and music education? Although many of the ideas found in Gould's writings are explored elsewhere, Gould presents a unique synthesis of thought that studies music's relationship to a person's spiritual development.

Gould's emphasis on spiritual phenomena is the basis for an epistemology based on intuitive knowing. It also presents a paradigm of the creative process that emanates from spiritual development factors for musicians. The model focuses on unself-conscious knowing, self-mastery, and also awards great importance to the concept of negation in creativity.

Music can be a vehicle for psychological and spiritual growth. Gould promotes the discovery of identity through music which empowers individuals to attain their full potential. Human psychic growth is fostered through the use of music as an intuitive mode.

The empirical approach to music education is in direct contrast to Gould's hypothesis that knowledge should be personal. Polanyi described the kind of personal knowledge Gould implied. Polanyi wrote,

> Such knowing is indeed objective in the sense of establishing contact with a hidden reality; a contact that is defined as the condition for anticipating an indeterminate range of yet unknown (and perhaps yet inconceivable) true implications. . . . It seems reasonable to describe this fusion of the personal and the objective as Personal Knowledge. (Polanyi, 1962, p. viii)

Gould detailed the ways in which music can assume moral and spiritual overtones. After reading his work, we know music in ways not usually presented in traditional literature and practice of music education. Gould uncovered that music could be a state of mind most conducive to peak experience, which are moments of great insight. In turn, music can be a facilitator to transformative ecstatic awareness. In an iconic sense, music can externally, symbolically manifest the conditions to self-actualization.

Gould reminds us that the highest morality for the musician is self-actualization. It is a wholeness of being, in harmony with the world, that demonstrates reverence for life and uses music as a tool to achieve this end.

Do we know anything more about Gould after reading his works? We know that Gould was not an example of a sick, eccentric personality, rather, just the opposite: a healthy, self-actualized person. Sinetar (1986) wrote that the healthiest personalities have much to teach us about how to be mature, generous, virtuous, and happy. We know that Gould's mind was a metaphorical mind. Through his complex metaphors we learn about aspects of his creative process, aspects of his self-actualization process, and aspects of his spiritual life. We also realize that Gould was a futurist in that he outlined a re-created world where creative openness can lead to utopian levels of consciousness.

It is illustrated in this book that Gould's thought is closely related to (1) *Marxist aesthetics* in addressing moral and social issues; (2) *Formalism* in stressing the formal, theoretical properties of music (Gould does not explore the ontological nature of music except to discuss music's formal properties); (3) *Phenomenology* in that one should detach oneself from the musical composition in order that the work can open to us: back to the things themselves; (4) *Existentialism* in that our knowledge of the world should be informed by the person. Each person is responsible to the world and must nurture self-actualization.

There are times in which one can see apparent contradictions in Gould's thought. He steadfastly defended the unconditional autonomy of the creative artist, and yet, simultaneously urged the artist to participate in shared work projects that facilitated anonymity.

He developed a complex plan for the musician to achieve self-actualization but insisted that self-actualization can only occur by abandoning the self through transcendence. His antihistorical (antichronological) stance affirmed the absolute reality of the immediate experience in music. However, his socio-musico arguments indicated a belief that music is of history and reflects the conflicts inherent in the social order.

Gould's leanings towards a morality of social conduct was countered by his existentialist (introspective) proclivities. Gould the puritanical censor offset Gould the totally free artist. Finally, Gould the recluse confronted Gould the world personality.

If taken literally, Gould's counterpoint of thought appears irreconcilable. But if viewed as a model of mind rooted in the creative process, we better understand that Gould had attempted to point through the contradictory tensions to a synthesis marked by moral struggle.

It would be a misjudgment if we were to assess Glenn Gould's contributions to a philosophy of music and music education solely in light of formal philosophical method. Gould was not a professional philosopher, and oftentimes deviated from the logical processes employed in philosophical inquiry.

In addition, one might be tempted to trivialize Gould's conclusions since they are existentialist in tone and sometimes echo popular cultural ideology from the 1960's to the present. The fact that Gould emphasized spiritual phenomena seems to be a part of that general mentality.

Rather, if we are to begin to understand Gould we must make a quantum leap beyond his field of contradictions and use of popular modes. We must focus on him as an artist preeminently reflective of the aesthetic climate of his time. Gould could be thought of as a modern-day John the Baptist heralding the incongruous spirit of contemporary music.

He championed anonymity, ecstasy, transcendence, and art-as-life in order to resolve his isolation, his estrangement from reality. He incisively penetrated the struggles and problems of alienation the modern musical artist faces. In doing so, he exchanged the fixed aesthetic category to replace it by an ethical one.

GLOSSARY

aesthetic—the branch of philosophy that explores the problems relating to art works and their significance

analytic formalist—theorist who holds that musical meaning is primarily intellectual

antimusic—a form of experimental music that denies traditional musical expression

axiological—dealing with value, its nature and types

congeneric—meanings of music's syntax

Dasein—human being in Heidegger's philosophical writings

designative meaning—nonmusical reactions to a musical composition

discursive language—language by which our knowledge is inferred. If one can verbalize a concept then discursive language is involved. It is the opposite of intuitive knowledge.

dodecaphonic—music composition using twelve-tone techniques

dynamic modulation—the process of changing dynamics

embodied meaning—musical expectations stimulated by music events

epistemology—the branch of philosophical inquiry that deals with knowledge

epoche—referring to the phenomenological epoche of Husserl, it is the suspension of judgment or the bracketing of experience in order to eliminate preconceptions

eschatology—branch of theology that speculates about final things, namely, death, the end of the world, final stages of the cosmos

extrageneric meaning—music's meaning outside of musical parameters

extramusical—outside of musical parameters

formalism—any intellectual paradigm that emphasizes form over content or meaning

German idealists—Fichte, Schelling, and Hegel represent the core of German idealism

gestalt—an integrated phenomenon

Gestalt theory of isomorphism—in Gestalt psychology the similarity of structure between brain fields and content of consciousness

hermeneutic—the process of interpreting

iconoclastic—attacking cherished beliefs

information theory—concerned with information caused by stimuli

isomorphism—sharing the same structure

klangfarbenmelodien—term meaning sound-color-melody; usually pointillistic, each pitch has a separate timbre

logical positivists—emphasize language analysis in the pursuit of meaning

Marxist-Hegelian dialectical method—the developmental process by which two opposites achieve a synthesis of higher value through contradiction

metatheoretical—a critical process that examines theory

musical gesture—a mode of action that carries musical meaning

musique concrète—the musical process by which nonsynthesized sounds are manipulated on recording tape

ontology—the study of being

pointillism—sounds separated by time and space

positivism—denies the existence of a reality beyond the scientific facts

referential meaning—meanings outside the object of focus

rhythmic modulation—the change of rhythmic ideas

rubric—a stylized rule of procedure

semantic—the signification or meaningful interpretation of signs and symbols

semblance—is a thing's direct aesthetic quality

semiotics—the theory of signs

spatial modulation—the apparent movement of sound through space

syntax—studies signs independently of their interpretation

systematic philosophy—is highly disciplined philosophical speculation that starts with propositions and ranks some facts over others

tabula rasa—the blank tablet of the mind; denies a priori knowledge

teleological—theory of final ends, goals, purposes

typology—classifying according to parts

utilitarian value—espouses the philosophical posture that one ought to act for the greatest good

virtual time—an image of time in a different mode

REFERENCES

References to works by Glenn Gould are listed separately, beginning on page 211.

Abeles, H., Hoffer, C., & Klotman, R. (1984). *Foundations of music education.* New York: Schirmer Books.

Ackerman, J.S. et al. (1981). Aesthetics and world-making: An exchange with Nelson Goodman. *The Journal of Aesthetics and Art Criticism, 39,* 249–280.

Adorno, T. (1967). *Prisms.* Translated from the German by Samuel and Shierry Weber. Cambridge: The M.I.T. Press.

———. (1973). *Philosophy of modern music.* Translated by Anne G. Mitchell and Wesley V. Blomster. New York: Continuum Publishing Company.

———. (1976). *Introduction to a sociology of music.* New York: Continuum Publishing Company.

Alperson, P. (1981). Schopenhauer and musical revelation. *The Journal of Aesthetics and Art Criticism, 40,* 155–166.

Anderson, J. C. (1982). Musical identity. *The Journal of Aesthetics and Art Criticism, 40,* 285–292.

———. (1985). Musical kinds. *The British Journal of Aesthetics, 25,* 43–49.

Arnheim, R. (1967). *Toward a psychology of art.* Berkeley and Los Angeles: University of California Press.

———. (1981). Style as a gestalt problem. *The Journal of Aesthetics and Art Criticism, 39* (3), 281–289.

Aspin, D. N. (1982). The place of music in the curriculum: A justification. *The Journal of Aesthetic Education, 16,* 41–56.

Austin, M. R. (1980). Aesthetic experience and the nature of religious perception. *The Journal of Aesthetic Education, 14* (3), 19–35.

Ballantine, C. (1983). *Twentieth-century symphony.* London: Dennis Dobson.

———. (1984). *Music and its social meanings.* New York: Gordon and Breach Science Publishers.

Ballard, E. G. (1978). *Man and technology: Toward the measurement of a culture*. Pittsburgh: Duquesne University Press.

Barnett, D. (1972). *The performance of music*. New York: Universe Books.

Barrett, C. (1982). The morality of artistic production. *The Journal of Aesthetics and Art Criticism, 41* (2), 137–144.

Beardsley, M. C. (1958). *Aesthetics: Problems in the philosophy of criticism*. New York: Harcourt, Brace and World, Inc.

———. (1966). *Aesthetics from classical Greece to the present*. New York: The Macmillan Company.

———. (1980). Review of E. Lippman, *A humanistic philosophy of music*. *The Musical Quarterly, 66* (2), 305–306.

———. (1981). Understanding music. In K. Price (ed.), *On criticizing music: Five philosophical perspectives* (pp. 55–73). Baltimore: The Johns Hopkins University Press.

Bennett, J. G. (1982). Review of N. Wolterstorff, *Works and worlds of art*. *The Journal of Aesthetics and Art Criticism, 40* (4), 431–433.

Bent, I. (1987). *Analysis*. New York: W. W. Norton & Company.

Bentley, A. (1975). *Music in education*. Windsor, Eng.: NFER Publishing Company, Ltd.

Bernstein, L. (1959). *The joy of music*. New York: New American Library, Signet Books.

———. (1976). *The unanswered question: Six talks at Harvard*. Cambridge: Harvard University Press.

———. (1983). The truth about a legend. In J. McGreevy (ed.), *Glenn Gould: Variations* (pp. 17–22). Toronto: Doubleday Canada Limited.

Bester, A. (1964, April). The zany genius of Glenn Gould. *Holiday, 150.*

Black, M. (ed.) (1964). *Philosophy in America*. Ithaca, N.Y.: Cornell University Press.

Block, E. (1985). *Essays on the philosophy of music*. Cambridge: Cambridge University Press.

Blum, F. (1959). *Susanne Langer's music aesthetics*. Unpublished doctoral dissertation, University of Iowa.

Blumenfeld, H. (1984). Ad vocem Adorno. *The Musical Quarterly, 70* (4), 515–537.

Boretz, B. & Cone, E. T. (eds.) (1971). *Perspectives on American composers*. New York: W. W. Norton and Company, Inc.

———. (1972). *Perspectives on contemporary music theory*. New York: W. W. Norton and Company, Inc.

———. (1976). *Perspectives on notation and performance*. New York: W. W. Norton and Company, Inc.

Bowman, W. D. (1982). Polanyi and instructional method in music. *The Journal of Aesthetic Education, 16,* 75–86.

Broder, N. (1956, February). Wunderkind among the Goldbergs. *High Fidelity/Musical America, 6,* 75.

Brook, B. S. (ed.) (1972). *Perspectives in musicology.* New York: W. W. Norton and Company, Inc.

Broudy, H. (1958). A realistic philosophy of music education. In N. Henry (ed.), *Basic concepts in music education* (pp. 62–87). Chicago: The National Society for the Study of Education.

Browne, R. (1981). *Music theory: Special topics.* New York: Academic Press.

Budd, M. (1980). The repudiation of emotion: Hanslick on music. *The British Journal of Aesthetics, 20,* 29–43.

Cage, J. (1961). *Silence.* Middletown, Conn.: Wesleyan University Press.

Callen, D. (1982). The sentiment in musical sensibility. *The Journal of Aesthetics and Art Criticism, 40,* 381–393.

Campbell, D. G. (1983). *Introduction to the musical brain.* Saint Louis: Magnamusic-Baton, Inc.

Cavell, S. (1964). Aesthetic problems of modern philosophy. In M. Black (ed.), *Philosophy in America* (pp. 74–97). Ithaca, N.Y.: Cornell University Press.

Choate, R. A. (ed.) (1968). *Documentary report of the Tanglewood symposium.* Washington, D.C.: Music Educators National Conference.

Christensen, J. (1984). The spiritual and the material in Schoenberg's thinking. *Music and Letters, 65* (4), 337–344.

Clark, A. (1982). Is music a language? *The Journal of Aesthetics and Art Criticism, 41,* 195–204.

Coker, W. (1972). *Music and meaning.* New York: The Free Press.

Collingwood, R. G. (1933). *An essay on philosophical method.* London: Oxford University Press.

Cook, N. (1987). *A guide to musical analysis.* New York: George Braziller.

Cooke, D. (1959). *The language of music.* Oxford: Oxford University Press.

———. (1982). *Vindications: Essays on romantic music.* Cambridge: Cambridge University Press.

Cooper, M. (1965). *Ideas and music.* Philadelphia and New York: Chilton Books, Publishers.

———. (ed.) (1974). *The modern age, 1890–1960.* Volume 10 of *The new Oxford history of music.* New York: Oxford University Press.

Copland, A. (1959). *Music and imagination.* New York: The New American Library of World Literature, Inc.

Cott, J. (1984). *Conversations with Glenn Gould.* Boston: Little, Brown, and Company.

Croce, B. (1970). *Aesthetic.* Translated from Italian by Douglas Ainslie. New York: Farrar, Straus, and Giroux.

Culver, A. G. (1973). *Theodor Adorno's philosophy of modern music: Evaluation and commentary.* Unpublished Ph.D. dissertation, University of Colorado.

Dahlhaus, C. (1982). *Esthetics of music.* Cambridge: Cambridge University Press.

———. (1983). *Analysis and value judgment.* Translated from the German by Siegmund Levarie. New York: Pendragon Press.

Dallin, L. (1974). *Techniques of twentieth century composition.* 3rd edition. Dubuque, Iowa: Wm. C. Brown.

Darack, D. (1964). Foreword to *Arnold Schoenberg: A perspective,* by Glenn Gould. Cincinnati: University of Cincinnati, Occasional Papers no. 3, p. 5.

DaSilva, F., Blasi, A., & Dees, D. (1984). *The sociology of music.* Notre Dame, Ind.: University of Notre Dame Press.

De Jager, H. (1974). Music regarded from a sociological point of view. *Music and Man, 1,* 161–167.

Dubal, D. (1984). *Reflections from the keyboard.* New York: Summit Books.

Dunsby, J. (1983, Winter). Music and semiotics: The Nattiez phase. *The Musical Quarterly, 69* (1), 22–43.

Dutton, D. (1979). A book review of *Glenn Gould: Music and mind. Journal of Aesthetics, 37* (4), 513.

Earhart, W. (1935). *The meaning and teaching of music.* New York: Witmark Educational Publishers.

Ecker, D. (ed.) (1981). *Qualitative evaluation in the arts.* New York: Division of Arts and Arts Education, New York University.

Ecker, D. W. & Kaelin, E. F. (1972). *The limits of aesthetic inquiry: A guide to educational research. Seventy-first yearbook of the National Society for the Study of Education* (pp. 258–286). Chicago: University of Chicago Press.

Eimert, H. & Stockhausen, K. (eds.) (1975). *Die Reihe: Young composers.* Translated by Leo Black. New Jersey: Universal Edition Publishing, Inc.

Eisner, E. W. (1985). *The educational imagination: On the design and evaluation of school programs.* 2nd edition. New York: Macmillan Publishing Company.

Epperson, G. (1967). *The musical symbol.* Ames: Iowa State University Press.

Ferguson, D. N. (1959). *A history of musical thought.* New York: Appleton-Century-Crofts.

———. (1960). *Music as metaphor: The elements of expression.* Minneapolis: University of Minnesota Press.

Ferrara, L. (1978). *Referential meaning in music.* Unpublished Ph.D. dissertation, New York University.

———. (1981). Allowing oneself to be moved: A phenomenology of musical evaluation. In D. W. Ecker (ed.), *Qualitative evaluation in the arts* (pp. 125–151). New York: Division of Arts and Arts Education, New York University.

———. (1982). Research and practice in music education: The problem of dislocation. *Journal of the College Music Society, 22* (1), 65–72.

———. (1984, Summer). Phenomenology as a tool for musical analysis. *The Musical Quarterly, 70* (3), 355–373.

Fisher, J. (ed.) (1983). *Essays on aesthetics.* Philadelphia: Temple University Press.

Ford, C. (1982). *Canada's music: An historical survey.* Agincourt, Ont.: G.L.C. Publishers Limited.

Foss, L. (1976). The changing composer-performer relationship: A monologue and a dialogue. In B. Boretz & E. T. Cone (eds.), *Perspectives on notation and performance* (pp. 32–40). New York: W. W. Norton and Company, Inc.

Fowler, C. (1988). Toward a democratic art: A reconstructionist view of music education. In T. Gates (ed.), *Music education in the United States: Contemporary Issues* (pp. 130–156). Tuscaloosa: University of Alabama Press.

French, P. A. (1979). *The scope of morality.* Minneapolis: University of Minnesota Press.

Fulford, R. (1983). Growing up Gould. In J. McGreevy (ed.), *Glenn Gould: Variations* (pp. 57–63). Toronto: Doubleday Canada Limited.

Gallwey, T. & Kriegel, B. (1977). *Inner skiing.* Toronto: Bantam Books.

Gardner, H. (1982). *Art, mind, and brain.* New York: Basic Books, Inc., Publishers.

———. (1983). *Frames of mind.* New York: Basic Books, Inc., Publishers.

Gates, T. (ed.) (1988). *Music education in the United States: Contemporary issues.* Tuscaloosa: University of Alabama Press.

Gelatt, R. (1956, April). Music makers. *High Fidelity/Musical America, 6,* 67, 69.

———. (1962, March). Music makers. *High Fidelity, 12* (13), 67.

Gerig, F. G. (1974). *Famous pianists and their technique*. Washington, D.C.: Robert B Luce, Inc.

Goldberg, P. (1983). *The intuitive edge*. Los Angeles: Jeremy P. Tarcher, Inc.

Goldsmith, H. (1983, February). Glenn Gould: An appraisal. *High Fidelity/Musical America, 33* (2), 54–55.

Goodman, A. H. (1982). *Music education: Perspectives and perceptions*. Dubuque, Iowa: Kendall Hunt Publishing Company.

Goodman, N. (1982). Implementation of the arts. *The Journal of Aesthetics and Art Criticism, 40* (3), 281–283.

Goolsby, T. W. (1984). Music education as aesthetic education: concepts and skills for the appreciation of music. *The Journal of Aesthetic Education, 18,* 15–34.

Gowin, D. & Dyason, D. (1984). On epistemology: Events, facts, and concepts. *The Journal of Aesthetic Education.* Vol. 18, #4, Winter.

Graf, M. (1946). *Composer and critic*. New York: W. W. Norton and Company, Inc.

Griffiths, P. (1981). *Modern music: The avant garde since 1945*. New York: George Braziller.

Gurney, E. (1880). *The power of sound*. London: Smith, Elder, and Company.

Haggin, B. H. (1984, August). Glenn Gould: A corrective assessment of the pianist's use of his phenomenal gifts. *High Fidelity/Musical America,* 39–42, 48.

Hanslick, E. (1957). *The beautiful in music*. Originally published in 1854. Translated by Gustav Cohen. Edited by Morris Weitz. New York: The Bobbs-Merrill Company, Inc.

Harrison, N. (1978). Creativity in musical performance. *The British Journal of Aesthetics, 18* (4), 300–306.

Heidegger, M. (1956). *What is philosophy?* Translated by Jean T. Wilde and William Kluback. New Haven, Conn.: The New College and University Press.

———. (1977). *The question concerning technology and other essays*. Translated by William Lovitt. New York: Harper and Row, Publishers.

Helm, E. (1970). *Composer, performer, public*. Florence: Leo S. Olschki.

Henry, N. (ed.) (1958). *Basic concepts in music education: The fifty-seventh yearbook of the National Society for the Study of Education*. Part I. Chicago: University of Chicago Press.

Hiemenz, J. (1984, February). Glenn Gould on film. *High Fidelity/Musical America, 34,* MA p. 2 + .

Hindemith, P. (1961). *A composer's world*. Garden City, N.Y.: Doubleday and Company, Inc.

Hoaglund, J. (1980). Music as expressive. *The British Journal of Aesthetics, 20,* 340–348.

Horton, J. (1950). *Approach to music*. London: George Allen and Unwin, Ltd.

Howes, F. (1970). *Man, mind, and music*. Freeport, N.Y.: Books for Libraries Press.

Hurwitz, R. (1983). Towards a contrapuntal radio. In J. McGreevy (ed.), *Glenn Gould: Variations* (pp. 253–263). Toronto: Doubleday Canada Limited.

Illich, I. (1971). *Deschooling society*. New York: Harper and Row, Publishers.

Irvine, D. B. (1945). *Methods of research in music*. Ann Arbor, Mich.: Edwards Brothers, Inc.

Ives, C. (1962). *Essays before a sonata*. New York: W. W. Norton and Company, Inc.

Johnson, P. (1984). *Marxist aesthetics: The foundations within everyday life for an emancipated consciousness*. London: Routledge & Kegan Paul.

Jorgensen, E. R. (1976). *A critical analysis of selected aspects of music education*. Unpublished doctoral dissertation, University of Calgary, Alta.

Karajan, H. von. (1983, October). From *Program notes* (p. 1). Glenn Gould film festival, Symphony Space, New York City.

Kassler, J. C. (1983). Heinrich Schenker's epistemology and philosophy of music: An essay on the relations between evolutionary theory and music theory. In D. Oldroyd & I. Langham (eds.), *The wider domain of evolutionary thought* (pp. 221–260). New York: D. Reidel Publishing Company.

Khatchadourian, H. (1980). Humanistic functions of the arts today. *The Journal of Aesthetic Education, 14* (2), 11–22.

Kivy, P. (1980). *The corded shell: Reflections on musical expression*. Princeton, N.J.: Princeton University Press.

Koscis, S. (1983, October). From *Program notes* (p. 9). Glenn Gould film festival, Symphony Space, New York City.

Kung, H. (1981). *Art and the question of meaning*. Translated by Edward Quinn. New York: Crossroad.

Kupperman, J. J. (1978). *Philosophy: The fundamental problems*. New York: St. Martin's Press.

Langer, S. K. (1942). *Philosophy in a new key*. Cambridge: Harvard University Press.

———. (1953). *Feeling and form*. New York: Charles Scribner's Sons.

————. (1961). *Reflections on art: A source book of writings by artists, critics and philosophers*. New York: Oxford University Press.

Lemmon, D. C. (1977). Strategy in Bennett Reimer's *A philosophy of music education*. *Council of Research on Music Education Bulletin, 51*, 1–9.

Leonard, G. B. (1968). *Education and ecstasy*. New York: Delacorte Press.

Leonhard, C. (1955, Spring). Research: Philosophy and esthetics. *Journal of Research in Music Education, 23*–26.

————. (1965). The philosophy of music education—present and future. In *Comprehensive musicianship: The foundation for college education in music* (pp. 42–49). Washington, D.C.: Contemporary Music Project/Music Educators National Conference.

Leonhard, C. & House, R. W. (1972). *Foundations and principles of music education*. New York: McGraw-Hill Book Company.

Lerdahl, F. & Jackendoff, R. (1983). *A generative theory of tonal music*. Cambridge: The M.I.T. Press.

Lévi-Strauss, C. (1970). *The raw and the cooked: Introduction to a science of mythology*. Vol. 1 translated by John Weightman. New York: Harper and Row.

Lewis, D. R. (1972). *Implications for music education from Susanne K. Langer, Abraham Maslow, Marshall McLuhan, Jerome S. Bruner, Max Kaplan, and Jean Piaget*. Unpublished doctoral thesis, University of Mississippi.

Lipman, M. (1973). *Contemporary aesthetics*. Boston: Allyn and Bacon, Inc.

Lippman, E. A. (1977). *A humanistic philosophy of music*. New York: New York University Press.

————. (1981). The dilemma of musical meanings. *International Review of Aesthetics and Sociology of Music, 12* (2), 181–202.

Littler, W. (1983). The quest for solitude. In J. McGreevy (ed.), *Glenn Gould: Variations* (pp. 217–224). Toronto: Doubleday Canada Limited.

Madeja, S. S. (1974). Aesthetic judgments as an outcome for education. *Music and Man, 1*, 239–244.

Mann, J. (1975). Music and stasis. *Music and Man, 1*, 305–317.

Mark, M. L. (1978). *Contemporary music education*. New York: Schirmer Books.

————. (1982). The evolution of music education philosophy from utilitarian to aesthetic. *The Journal of Research in Music Education, 30* (1), 15–21.

————. (1982). *Source readings in music education history*. New York: Schirmer Books.

————. (1988). Aesthetics and utility reconciled: The importance to society of education in music. In T. Gates (ed.), *Music education in the United States: Contemporary issues* (pp. 111–129). Tuscaloosa: University of Alabama Press.

Maslow, A. H. (1968). *Toward a psychology of being.* 2nd edition. New York: Van Nostrand Reinhold Company.

————. (1971). *The farther reaches of human nature.* New York: Penguin Books.

Mason, J. A., Lehmann, P., & McKeachie, W. J. (1981). *Documentary report of the Ann Arbor symposium.* Reston, Va.: Music Educators National Conference.

McGreevy, J. (ed.) (1983). *Glenn Gould: Variations.* Toronto: Doubleday Canada Limited.

McKay, G. (1958). The range of musical experience. In N. Henry (ed.), *Basic concepts in music education* (pp. 123–139). Chicago: University of Chicago Press.

McLuhan, M. (1964). *Understanding media: The extensions of man.* New York: McGraw-Hill Book Company.

McLuhan, M. & Leonard, G. (1969). Learning in the global village. In R. & G. Gross (eds.), *Radical school reform* (p. 106). New York: Simon and Schuster.

McMurray, F. (1958). Pragmatism in music education. In N. Henry, (ed.), *Basic concepts in music education* (pp. 30–61). Chicago: University of Chicago Press.

Menuhin, Y. (1983). Glenn Gould: The creator. In J. McGreevy (ed.), *Glenn Gould: Variations* (pp. 303–305). Toronto: Doubleday Canada Limited.

Mertens, W. (1983). *American minimal music.* London: Kahn and Averill.

Mew, P. (1985). The expression of emotion in music. *The British Journal of Aesthetics, 25* (1), 33–41.

Meyer, L. (1956). *Emotion and meaning in music.* Chicago: University of Chicago Press.

————. (1967). *Music, the arts and ideas.* Chicago: University of Chicago Press.

————. (1973). *Explaining music.* Chicago: University of Chicago Press.

————. (1975–1976). Grammatical simplicity and relational richness: The trio of Mozart's G minor symphony. *Critical Inquiry, 2,* 693–694.

————. (1979). The dilemma of choosing: Speculations about contemporary culture. In E. Maziarz (ed.), *Value and values in evolution: A symposium* (pp. 136–137). New York: Gordon and Breach.

Monsaingeon, B. (producer, director) (1981). *The Goldberg Variations* [Film]. Paris, France, Clasart Films.

Moran, G. (1987). No ladder to the sky. San Francisco: Harper & Row.

Morgan, R. (1973, February). Glenn Gould, extraordinary harpsichordist. *High Fidelity/Musical America, 23,* 84.

Morgenstern, S. (ed.) (1956). *Composers on music.* New York: Pantheon Books, Inc.

Morton, B. N. (1971). *Some problems in the philosophy of music.* Unpublished Ph.D. dissertation, University of Rochester.

Murphy, J. (1980). Conflict, consensus, and communication: An interpretive report on the application of psychology to the teaching and learning of music. *Music Educator's Journal,* S-2 to S-32.

Murphy, J. & Sullivan, G. (1968). *Music in American society.* Washington, D.C.: Music Educators National Conference.

Mursell, J. (1934). *Human values in music education.* New York: Silver Burdett Co.

———. (1948). *Education for musical growth.* New York: Ginn and Company.

———. (1958). Growth processess in music education. In N. Henry, (ed.), *Basic concepts in music education* (pp. 140–162). Chicago: University of Chicago Press.

———. (1965). *Music education: Principles and programs.* New York: Silver Burdett Co.

Nattiez, J.-J. (1975). *Fondements d'une sémiologie de la musique.* Paris, France: Union générale d'éditions.

Newman, A. J. (1980). Aesthetic sensitizing and moral education. *The Journal of Aesthetic Education, 14* (12), 93–101.

Ogden, C. K. & Richards, I. A. (1946). *The meaning of meaning.* With supplementary essays by B. Malinowski and F. G. Crookshank. 8th edition. New York: Harcourt, Brace, and World, Inc.

Oldenquist, A. (ed.) (1965). *Readings in moral philosophy.* Boston: Houghton Mifflin Company.

Oldroyd, D. & Langham, I. (eds.) (1983). *The wider domain of evolutionary thought.* New York: D. Reidel Publishing Company.

Osborne, H. (1982). Expressiveness in the arts. *The Journal of Aesthetics and Art Criticism, 41,* 19–26.

Page, T. (1981). Glenn Gould. *The Piano Quarterly, 115,* 14.

Page, T. & Said, E. W. (1983, May). Glenn Gould: Private in public. *Vanity Fair, 46* (3), 97–128.

Payzant, G. (1978). *Glenn Gould: Music and mind.* Toronto: Van Nostrand Reinhold Ltd.

Phelps, R. P. (1980). *A guide to research in music education.* Metuchen, N.J.: Scarecrow Press.

Pike, A. (1953). *A theology of music.* Toledo, Ohio: The Gregorian Institute of America.

Polanyi, M. (1962). *Personal knowledge: Towards a post-critical philosophy.* Chicago and London: University of Chicago Press.

Polanyi, M. & Prosch, H. (1975). *Meaning.* Chicago and London: University of Chicago Press.

Portnoy, J. (1954). *The philosopher and music.* New York: The Humanities Press.

———. (1963). *Music in the life of man.* New York: Holt, Rinehart and Winston.

Prall, D. W. (1929). *Aesthetic judgment.* New York: Thomas Y. Crowell Company.

———. (1936). *Aesthetic analysis.* New York: Thomas Y. Crowell Company.

Pratt, C. C. (1931). *The meaning of music.* New York: McGraw-Hill Book Company, Inc.

Price, K. (ed.) (1981). Introduction. In *On criticizing music: Five philosophical perspectives* (pp. 1–15). Baltimore: The Johns Hopkins University Press.

Proctor, G. (1980). *Canadian music of the twentieth century.* Toronto: University of Toronto Press.

Rachels, J. (ed). (1971). *Moral problems.* New York: Harper and Row, Publishers.

Rahn, J. (1983). *A theory for all music: Problems and solutions in the analysis of non-western forms.* Toronto: University of Toronto Press.

Reese, S. (1980). Polanyi's tacit knowing and music education. *The Journal of Aesthetic Education, 14,* 75–89.

Reid, L. A. (1941). Knowing in music. *Aristotlean Society, 41,* 113–126.

Reimer, B. (1970). *A philosophy of music education.* Englewood Cliffs, N.J.: Prentice-Hall, Inc.

———. (1977). Language and nonlanguage models of aesthetic stimuli. *The Journal of Aesthetic Education, 11,* 37–48.

Robbins, L. B. (1985). *Waking up! In the age of creativity.* Sante Fe, N. Mex.: Bear & Company.

Roberts, J. (1983, October). A tribute. From *Program notes* (p. 8). Glenn Gould film festival, Symphony Space, New York City.

Rochberg, G. (1979). *The aesthetics of survival*. Ann Arbor: The University of Michigan Press.

Roddy, J. (1983). Apollonian. In J. McGreevy (ed.), *Glenn Gould: Variations* (pp. 95–123). Toronto: Doubleday Canada Limited.

Rothenberg, A. (1979, June). Creative contradictions. *Psychology Today*, 55–62.

Rowell, L. (1983). *Thinking about music*. Amherst: The University of Massachusetts Press.

Russell, C. T. (1972). The analysis and evaluation of music: A philosophical inquiry. *The Musical Quarterly, 58* (2), 161–184.

Said, E. (1983). The music itself: Glenn Gould's contrapuntal vision. In J. McGreevy (ed.), *Glenn Gould: Variations* (pp. 45–54). Toronto: Doubleday Canada Limited.

Samuelson, W. (1988). *An introduction to philosophy in education*. New York: Philosophical Library.

Schafer, R. M. (1965). *The composer in the classroom*. Scarborough, Ont.: Berandol Music Limited.

———. (1967). *Ear cleaning*. Scarborough, Ont.: Berandol Music Limited.

———. (1969). *The new soundscape*. Scarborough, Ont.: Berandol Music Limited.

———. (1970). *When words sing*. Scarborough, Ont.: Berandol Music Limited.

———. (1977). *The tuning of the world*. New York: Alfred A. Knopf.

Schantz, A. P. (1983).*A new statement of values for music education based on the writings of Dewey, Meyer, and Wolterstorff*. Unpublished Ph.D. dissertation, University of Colorado.

Schnabel, A. (1933). *Reflections on music*. Manchester, Eng.: Manchester University Press.

Schoen, M. (1972). *The effects of music according to Plato and Aristotle*. Unpublished Ph.D. dissertation, Laval University.

Schoen-Nazzaro, M. B. (1978). Plato and Aristotle on the ends of music. *Laval Théologique Philosophique, 34* (3), 261–273.

Schueller, H. M. (1977). The aesthetic implications of avant-garde music. *The Journal of Aesthetics and Art Criticism, 35*, 397–410.

Schultz, A. (1963, May–June). Contest standards—are they logical? *The Piano Teacher, 5* (5), 6.

Schwadron, A. A. (1964, May). Aesthetic values in music education. *Music Journal, 42*.

————. (1965, February–March). Musical aesthetics: a review and critique. *Music Educators Journal, 51,* 62–64.

————. (1967). *Aesthetics: Dimensions for music education.* Washington, D.C.: Music Educators National Conference.

————. (1972). On play and music: A critique. *The Journal of Aesthetic Education, 6* (4), 11–24.

————. (1973). Comparative music aesthetics: Toward a universality of musicality. *Music and Man, 1,* 17–31.

————. (1973). Philosophy in music education: State of the research. *Council Research in Music Education, 34,* 41–53.

————. (1977). Philosophy and the teacher of music. *College Music Symposium, 17* (1), 74–81.

Scruton, R. (1983). *The aesthetic understanding.* New York: Methuen & Company.

Serafine, M. L. (1980). Against music as communication. *The Journal of Aesthetic Education, 14,* 85–96.

Sessions, R. (1971). *The musical experience of composer, performer, listener.* Princeton, N.J.: Princeton University Press.

————. (1979). *Roger Sessions on music.* Edited by Edward T. Cone. Princeton, N.J.: Princeton University Press.

Siegmeister, E. (1938). *Music and society.* New York: Critics Group Press.

Silva, J. & Miele, P. (1977). *The Silva mind control method.* New York: Pocket Books.

Silverman, R. (1983). Memories: Glenn Gould, 1932–1982. In J. McGreevy (ed.), *Glenn Gould: Variations* (pp. 143–149). Toronto: Doubleday Canada Limited.

Sinetar, M. (1986). *Ordinary people as monks and mystics.* New York: Paulist Press.

Skarda, C. A. (1979). Alfred Schultz's phenomenology of music. *Journal of Musicological Research, 3,* 75–132.

Skelton, R. A. (1976). *Weinzweig, Gould, Schafer: Three Canadian string quartets.* Unpublished D.M.A. dissertation, Indiana University.

Smith, F. J. (1973). Aesthetic re-education. *Music and Man, 1,* 73–88.

————. (ed.) (1976). *In search of musical method.* London: Gordon and Breach.

————. (1976). Music theory and the history of ideas. *Music and Man, 2,* 125–150.

————. (1979). *The experiencing of musical sound.* New York: Gordon and Breach.

Sparshott, F. (1980). Aesthetics of music. In S. Sadie (ed.), *The new grove dictionary of music and musicians: Vol. I* (pp. 120–135). London: Macmillan.

Stecker, R. (1984). Expression of emotion in (some of) the arts. *The Journal of Aesthetics and Art Criticism, 42,* 409–418.

Stravinsky, I. & Craft, R. (1947). *Poetics of music in the form of six lessons.* New York: Random House.

———. (1960). *Memories and commentaries.* Berkeley and Los Angeles: University of California Press.

———. (1962). *Expositions and developments.* Berkeley and Los Angeles: University of California Press.

Subotnik, R. R. (1981). Romantic music as post-Kantian critique: Classicism, romanticism, and the concept of the semiotic universe. In K. Price (ed.), *On criticizing music: Five philosophical perspectives* (pp. 74–98). Baltimore: The Johns Hopkins University Press.

Swanger, D. (1985). Moral and aesthetic judging. *Educational Theory, 35* (1), 85–96.

Tait, M. & Haack, P. (1984). *Principles and processes of music education.* New York: Teacher's College Press, Columbia University.

Tillich, P. (1952). *The courage to be.* New Haven and London: Yale University Press.

Tischler, H. (1974). A proposal for a multi-relational aesthetics. *International Review of Aesthetics and Sociology of Music, 3* (2), 140–151.

Tomas, V. (1962). The concept of expression in art. In J. Margolis (ed.), *Philosophy looks at the Arts* (pp. 30–45). New York: Charles Scribner's Sons.

Tovell, V. (producer) & Till, E. (producer) (1985). *Glenn Gould: A portrait* [Film]. Canadian Broadcasting Corporation.

Urdang, L. & Flexner, S. B. (eds.) (1968). *The Random House dictionary of the English language.* New York: Random House.

Vos Fellman, P. (1980). Constructing a philosophical paradigm for music education. *The Journal of Aesthetic Education, 14* (3), 37–50.

Wade, R. E. (1965). *Susanne K. Langer's musical aesthetics with implications for music education.* Unpublished Ed.D. dissertation, Indiana University.

Wait, M. (1986, Fall). Glenn Gould: Did we really hear him? *The Piano Quarterly,* 60–63.

Walker, R. (1984). *Music education: Tradition and innovation.* Springfield, Ill.: Charles C. Thomas, Publisher.

Walter, A. (1957). Music in a technological age. *Canadian Music Journal I, 3,* 5.

Weitz, M. (1956). The role of theory in aesthetics. *The Journal of Aesthetics and Art Criticism, 15,* 27–35.

———. (1959). *Problems in aesthetics.* New York: The Macmillan Company.

Weitzman, R. (1971). An introduction to Adorno's music and social criticism. *Music and Letters,* 287–298.

Wilson, J., Cowell, B., Gowin, D. B., & Dyason, D. (1984). Knowledge and the humanities: The continuing debate. *The Journal of Aesthetic Education, 18* (4), 77–94.

Winking, J. L. (1980). Beardsley's aesthetics, musical analysis, and musical listening. *Journal of Aesthetic Education, 14,* 91–103.

Wreen, M. J. & Callen, D. M. (eds.) (1982). *The aesthetic point of view.* Ithaca, N.Y.: Cornell University Press.

Youngblood, J. (1958). Style as information. *Journal of Music Theory, 2,* 24.

Youngren, W. (1983, January). Interpreting Glenn Gould. *The Atlantic Monthly,* 96–100.

WORKS BY GLENN GOULD

GGC in references denotes Glenn Gould Collection of the National Library of Canada, Ottawa.

Undated. Anthology of variation. T.V. script. GGC.

Undated. Artist as artisan. Media script. GGC.

Undated. Glenn Gould interviewed by Andrew Marshall. Media script, p. 21. GGC.

Undated. Glenn Gould interviewed by Bernard Asbell. Media transcript. GGC.

Undated. Glenn Gould on Closed-Circuit T.V.—Part Three. Media script. GGC.

Undated. Grieg/Bizet album. Notes from M32340.

Undated. The musical life of the future. Media script. Radio Diffusion, Télévision Française. GGC.

Undated. Prokofiev and Scriabin album. Notes from MS 7173.

Undated. Terry Riley. CBC radio broadcast. GGC.

Undated. The world of music #2: I solisti di Zagreb. T.V. script. GGC.

Undated. The world of music #3: The Boston Symphony at Tanglewood. T.V. script. GGC.

Undated. The world of music #4: Von Karajan–New World Symphony. T.V. script. GGC.

Undated. The world of music #5: Willan–Messiaen. T.V. script.
GGC.

Undated. The world of music #7: Abduction from the Seraglio.
T.V. script. GGC.

(1951). CBC startime. Script. GGC.

(1953a). A consideration of Anton Webern. Notes for new music
associates concert, Royal Conservatory of Music, Toronto,
pp. 1–4. GGC.

(1953b). Schoenberg piano concerto. Lecture transcript. December 17, 1953. GGC.

(1956a, Autumn). A dodecaphonist's dilemma. *Canadian Music
Journal*, (1), 20–29.

(1956b). Beethoven's last three piano sonatas. Notes from
Columbia ML 5130.

(1956c). Beethoven Sonatas #30, 31, 32. Notes from ML 5130.

(1956d, July 7) Glenn Gould. *The Toronto Telegram Weekend
Magazine, 6* (27), 6–11.

(1956e, July 9). Music of Sweelinck, Krenek, Gould, Schoenberg,
Berg. Notes for the Stratford festival concert, Festival
Theatre, Stratford, Ontario. GGC.

(1956f). The Goldberg variations. Notes from Columbia ML
5060.

(1957). Beethoven Concerto #2 & Bach Concerto #1. Notes
from ML 5211.

(1958a). Piano music of Berg, Schoenberg, and Krenek. Notes
from ML 5336.

(1958b). Beethoven and Bach Concerti. Notes from Columbia
ML 5298.

(1959a, March 28). I'm a child of nature. *Toronto Daily Star,* 150.

(1959b, November 26, 28). Schoenberg concerto for piano and
orchestra, op. 42. Notes for Cleveland orchestra subscrip-
tion concert, Severance Hall, Cleveland, Ohio, pp. 247–252.
GGC.

(1960a, November 26). Bodky on Bach. *Saturday Review, 43,* 48,
55.

(1960b, October 2). On Schoenberg. Notes for Vancouver
international festival, Vancouver, British Columbia, pp.
76–78. GGC.

(1960c). Gould's string quartet, op. 1. Notes from Columbia MS
6178.

(1961). Universality of Bach. Lecture transcript, pp. 1–8. GGC.

(1962a, March). An argument for Richard Strauss. *High Fidelity,
12,* 46–49 + .

(1962b). Enoch Arden. Notes from Columbia MS 6341.

(1962c). Glenn Gould on Strauss. T.V. script. GGC.

(1962d). Hindemith, the early years. Notes for Stratford festival concert, Festival Theatre, Stratford, Ontario (July 29). GGC.

(1962e, February). Let's ban applause. *Musical America, 82,* 10–11, 38–39.

(1962f). N'aimez-vous pas Brahms? Notes for the Baltimore symphony orchestra concert, Lyric Theater, Baltimore, Maryland (Oct. 9, 10). GGC.

(1962g). Piano concertos by Mozart and Schoenberg. Notes from Columbia MS 6339.

(1962h). The Schoenberg heritage. Notes for the Stratford festival concert, Stratford, Ontario (July 13, 15). GGC.

(1963a, July 28). Russian concert. Notes for Stratford festival concert, Festival Theatre, Stratford, Ontario. GGC.

(1963b). Schoenberg: Piano Concerto Op. 42. Notes for the San Francisco Symphony concert (Feb. 13–15). GGC.

(1963c). Strauss–Schoenberg concert. Notes for Stratford Festival Concert, Festival Theatre, Stratford, Ontario (July 21). GGC.

(1964a, December). An argument for music in the electronic age. *Varsity Graduate, 26–27,* 114–128.

(1964b). *Arnold Schoenberg: A perspective.* Cincinnati, Ohio: University of Cincinnati.

(1964c). Glenn Gould interviewed by Pat Moore for the CBC International Service, Dec. 15, 1964. GGC.

(1964d). Music in the Soviet Union. Lecture transcript. GGC.

(1964e). So you want to write a fugue? *Hi Fi Stereo Review, 12* (4), 51–55.

(1964f). Strauss and the electronic future. *Saturday Review, 47* (22), 58–59, 72.

(1964g). The history of the piano sonata. Lecture transcript (Feb. 2). GGC.

(1964h). The music of Proteus: Being some notes on the subjective character of fugal form. *Hi Fi Stereo Review, 12* (4), 48–50, 53–54.

(1964i). Transcript of a lecture presented at the University of Toronto. GGC.

(1965a, April). Dialogue on the prospects of recording. *University of Toronto Varsity Graduate, 11,* 50–62.

(1965b, December). L'esprit de jeunesse, et de corps, et d'art. *High Fidelity/Musical America, 15,* 188–190. Under the pseudonym Dr. Herbert von Hockmeister.

(1965c). McLuhan interviewed by Glenn Gould. Media script. GGC.

(1965d, August). Of time and time beaters. *High Fidelity/Musical America*, 136–137. Under the pseudonym Dr. Herbert von Hockmeister.

(1965e). Schoenberg's piano music. Notes from M2S736.

(1965f, March). The CBC: Camera wise. *High Fidelity/Musical America*, *15*, 86P–86Q. Under the pseudonym Dr. Herbert von Hockmeister.

(1965g, July). The Ives fourth. *High Fidelity/Musical America*, *15*, 96–97.

(1966a). CBC recital script. Remarks on Hindemith and Mozart, November 29, 1966. GGC.

(1966b). The aftermath of Breton. Media script. GGC.

(1966c, April). The prospects of recording. *High Fidelity/Musical America*, *16*, 46–63.

(1966d). The psychology of improvisation. CBC radio broadcast. GGC.

(1966e, December). We, who are about to be disqualified, salute you. *High Fidelity/Musical America*, *16*, MA 23–24, 30.

(1966f, December). Yehudi Menuhin: Musician of the year. *High Fidelity/Musical America*, *16*, 7–9.

(1967a). Arnold Schoenberg's Chamber Symphony #2. Notes from Columbia M2S 709.

(1967b). Canadian piano music in the twentieth century. Notes from CBS 32110046.

(1967c). The idea of north: An introduction. Liner notes from CBC Learning Systems, T-56997.

(1967d, November). The search for Petula Clark. *High Fidelity/Musical America*, *17*, 67–71.

(1967–1968). The idea of north. CBC publications, disc PR—8. GGC.

(1968a). Domenico Scarlatti. CBC broadcast. GGC.

(1968b). Lizst Transcription of Beethoven's Fifth Symphony. Notes from Columbia MS 7095.

(1968c, December). The record of the decade, according to a critic who should know, is Bach played on, of all things, a Moog synthesizer. *Saturday Night, 83*, 52, 54.

(1968d). The world of music #1: Majesty in Mantua. T.V. script. GGC.

(1968–1969). The latecomers. CBC publications, disc PR—9. GGC.

(1969a, April). Oh, for heaven's sake, Cynthia, there must be something else on. *High Fidelity/Musical America, 19*, MA–13, 14, 28.

(1969b). Piano Sonatas by Scriabin and Prokofiev. Notes from Columbia MS 7173.

(1969c, November 23). Should we dig up the rare romantics? *The New York Times,* 72–76.

(1969d). The latecomers: An introduction. Liner notes from CBC Learning Systems, T-57000.

(1969e). The well-tempered listener. Glenn Gould interviewed by C. Davis. Media script. GGC.

(1970a, June 6). Admit it, Mr. Gould, you have doubts about Beethoven. *The Globe and Mail Magazine,* 6–9.

(1970b). Beethoven's Pathétique, Moonlight, and Appassionata Sonatas. Notes from Columbia MS 7413.

(1970c). Beethoven Piano Sonatas, #8, 14, 23. Notes from Columbia MS 7413.

(1970d). His country's most experienced hermit chooses a desert-island discography. *High Fidelity* 29–32.

(1970e). Rosemary's babies? A humble British housewife transcribes compositions from dead composers. *High Fidelity/Musical America, 20,* 87–88 + .

(1971a, November). Gould quizzed. *American Guild of Organists and Royal Canadian College of Organists, 5,* 31–32.

(1971b). Pavan and Galliard. Notes from Columbia M 30825.

(1971c, Spring–Summer) Radio as music: Glenn Gould in conversation with John Jessop. *Canadian Music Book, 2,* 13–30.

(1972a, Fall). Glenn Gould interviews himself about Beethoven. *The Piano Quarterly, 79,* 2–5.

(1972b). The film Slaughterhouse Five. CBC radio broadcast, August 1972. GGC.

(1973a). Hindemith: Kommt seine zeit (wieder)? Translated into English by Peter Mueller, *Hindemith-Jahrbuch, 3,* 131–136.

(1973b). Hindemith: Will his time come? again? Notes from Columbia M 32350.

(1973c). Piano music by Grieg and Bizet, with a confidential caution to critics. Notes from Columbia M 32040.

(1973d). The age of ecstasy. Media script. GGC.

(1974a). Data bank on the upward-scuttling Mahler. *The Piano Quarterly, 22* (85), 19–21.

(1974b, February). Glenn Gould interviews Glenn Gould about Glenn Gould. *High Fidelity/Musical America,* 72–78.

(1974c). Korngold and the crisis of the piano sonata. Notes from Genesis GS 1055.

(1974d). Take two: Conference at Port Chillkoot. *The Piano Quarterly, 22* (86), 25–28.

(1974e). The future and "flat-foot floogie." *The Piano Quarterly*, *22* (87), 11, 12, 14.

(1974f, July 20). Today, simply politics and prejudices in America c. 1970 . . . but for time-capsule scholars it's Babbitt vs. flat-foot floogie. *Toronto Globe and Mail*, 6–9.

(1975a). An epistle to the Parisians: Music and technology. *The Piano Quarterly, 23,* 17–19.

(1975b, Winter). A festschrift for "Ernst who??" *The Piano Quarterly, 24,* 44–47.

(1975c, February 15). Glenn Gould talks Bach. *Toronto Star,* 5–8.

(1975d, July 19). Krenek, the prolific, is probably best known to the public at large as—Ernst who? *Toronto Globe and Mail.*

(1975e, August). The grass is always greener in the outtakes. *High Fidelity/Musical America, 25,* 54–58.

(1975f). Old faces, old forms. Media script. GGC.

(1975g). Quiet in the land. Radio documentary script. GGC.

(1976a, May 29). Bach to Bach (and belly to belly). *The Toronto Globe and Mail,* 4–6.

(1976b). Boulez. *The New Republic, 175* (26), 23–25.

(1976c, Summer). Fact, fancy, or psychohistory: Notes from the P.D.Q. underground. *The Piano Quarterly, 24,* 40–43.

(1976d, May). Streisand as Schwarzkopf. *High Fidelity 26,* 73–75.

(1976e, Fall). Take eight: Of Mozart and related matters. *The Piano Quarterly, 24,* 12–14+.

(1976f, March 8). Menuhin notes for CBC. GGC.

(1977a, February 26). Critics. *The Canadian,* 27–30.

(1977b). Criticizing the critics. Media script. GGC.

(1977c). Take 10—Stokowski in six scenes. *The Piano Quarterly, 26,* 7–10.

(1977d). Sibelius and the post-romantic piano style. *The Piano Quarterly, 25,* 22–27.

(1977e). Sibelius and the post-romantic style. Notes from CBC M 34555.

(1977f). Promos for the national radio competition for young composers. GGC.

(1977g). Stokowski memorial. Media script. GGC.

(1978a). A tale of two Marienlebens. Notes from CBS MZ 34597.

(1978b). Book review of Geoffrey Payzant's *Glenn Gould: Music and mind. The Piano Quarterly, 103,* 15–17.

(1978c). Glenn Gould interviewed by A. Marshall. Media script. GGC.

(1978d, March 27). Goddard as mid-Atlantic man. Media script. GGC.

(1978e, March 18). Portrait of a cantankerous composer. *Toronto Globe and Mail*, 2–7.

(1978f). Promos for national radio competition for young composers. GGC.

(1978g). Sviatoslav Richter. Media script. GGC.

(1978h, September 22). Telephone conversation with Oliver Daniel. Transcript. GGC.

(1979a). A hawk, a dove and a rabbit called Franz Joseph. *The Piano Quarterly, 105*, 44–47.

(1979b). Glenn Gould: Music and mind. *Music Educator's Journal, 66*, 84–85.

(1979c). Glenn Gould plays Bach: The essentials of Bach's keyboard output. Media scripts for a series of five video programs. GGC.

(1979d). Mozart: A personal view. Media script. GGC.

(1979e). Richard Strauss: The bourgeois hero. Media script. GGC.

(1980a). Memories of maude harbour or variations on a theme of Arthur Rubinstein. *The Piano Quarterly, 110*, 27–30.

(1980b, August). Glenn Gould interviewed by James Aiken. Media script. GGC.

(1980c, October). Mostly music: A conversation with Barclay McMillan. Media script. GGC.

(1980d). Glenn Gould interviewed by Elye Mach. Media transcript. GGC.

(1980e). Gould-McMillan interview. Media script. GGC.

(1981, Fall). Glenn Gould in conversation with Tim Page. *The Piano Quarterly, 115*, 14, 16, 18, 20–24.

(1982a, November) Gould in conversation with the editor. *Clavier*, 8.

(1982b). Glenn Gould on recording. CBS media script. GGC.

(1982c, March). Glenn Gould joue Bach: Extraits des conversations. Une production Clasart Films. Une série de trois films présentée et réalisée par Bruno Monsaingeon. GGC.

(1982d). Glenn Gould–Tim Page interview. Media script. GGC.

(& Davis, C., 1983a). The well-tempered listener. In J. McGreevy (ed.), *Glenn Gould: Variations* (pp. 275–294). Toronto: Doubleday Canada Limited.

(1983b). Stokowski in six scenes. In J. McGreevy (ed.), *Glenn Gould: Variations* (pp. 151–185). Toronto: Doubleday Canada Limited.

(1983c, January). What the recording process means to me. *High Fidelity/Musical America, 33*, 56–57.

(1984a). Music in the Soviet Union. In T. Page (ed.), *The Glenn Gould reader* (pp. 166–184). New York: Alfred A. Knopf.

(1984b). The psychology of improvisation. In T. Page (ed.), *The Glenn Gould reader* (pp. 255–257). New York: Alfred A. Knopf.

(1984c). Advice to a graduation. In T. Page (ed.), *The Glenn Gould reader* (pp. 3–7). New York: Alfred A. Knopf.

(1984d). Music and technology. In T. Page (ed.), *The Glenn Gould reader* (pp. 353–357). New York: Alfred A. Knopf.

(1984e). N'aimez-vous pas Brahms? In T. Page (ed.), *The Glenn Gould reader* (pp. 70–72). New York: Alfred A. Knopf.

NAME INDEX

SUBJECT INDEX